# TARGET: AMERICA

D1259962

# TARGET: AMERICA

*Hitler's Plan to Attack the United States*

JAMES P. DUFFY

LYONS PRESS
Guilford, Connecticut
*An imprint of Globe Pequot Press*

*for Kathy*

Copyright © 2004, 2006, 2012 by James P. Duffy
First Lyons Press paperback edition, 2006

**Target: America: Hitler's Plan to Attack the United States, by James P. Duffy,** was originally
published in hard cover by Praeger, an imprint of ABC-CLIO, LLC, Santa Barbara, CA. Copyright
© 2004 by James P. Duffy. Paperback edition by arrangement with ABC-CLIO, LLC. All rights
reserved.

Lyons Press is an imprint of Globe Pequot Press.

The Library of Congress has previously cataloged an earlier hardcover edition as follows:

Duffy, James P., 1941
    Target: America : Hitler's plan to attack the United States / James P. Duffy.
        p. cm.
    Includes bibliographical references and index.
    ISBN 0-275-96684-4 (alk. paper)
    1. World War, 1939-1945—Germany. 2. World War, 1939-1945—Campaigns—
United States. 3. Military weapons—Germany—History—20th century. 4. Airplanes,
Military—Germany—History—20th century. I. Title.
    D757.D754 2004
    940.54'013'0943—dc22

                                                                    2003064907

ISBN 978-0-7627-7292-6

Printed in the United States of America

10 9 8 7 6 5 4 3 2 1

# CONTENTS

# ACKNOWLEDGMENTS

MANY PEOPLE CONTRIBUTED TO THIS BOOK IN MANY DIFFERENT WAYS. I have thanked each of them at the time of their assistance, and want to thank them all here once again. Their names appear here in no specific order, and I hope I have not inadvertently missed anyone. All of the following contributed in some way, some small, others larger, to this book, although none are responsible for what I have done with the information or insights they shared with me.

First must be writer Frank Joseph, who originally aroused my interest in the entire subject of Axis planned attacks on the United States. I am also in debt to Jean Martin, PhD, for introducing me to Colonel Schwenke's plan; author David Kahn for sharing with me his Schwenke interview; Bob Waddell, Bob Widmer, and Gerry Trampler for their help with translations; Dan Johnson, whose Luft '46 website provided much information on advanced aircraft; Dr. Richard R. Muller of the USAF Air Command and Staff College; historian Dr. Gerhard Weinberg of the University of North Carolina; Sandy Donellan; William Beigel; Anne Angstadt; David Westwood; Marc James Small; Steven Zoraster; author Jack Olsen; Jim Bloom; Charles Bain; Scott Vanaken; Gregg Voss; Daniel Green; Mark Sansom; Matthias Simon; Erik Lund; David Irving; Ray A. K. Crawford; Albert A. Nofi; Nick Spark; Mike George; Bob Waldeck; Joe Brennan; Tom Roseland; Bob Truax; Bud Meyer; Tracy Dungan of V2rocket.com; Phil Broad; Gary Webster of germanvtol.com; Mark Wade of astronautix.com; and the various members of the H-WAR Discussion Network who have shared their knowledge and views with me.

I am also indebted to Giorgio Apostolo of *Aerofan;* David Myhra; TSgt Yancy Mailes; Ranieri Meloni; James S. Peters; Bill Beggs; George Mindling; Martyn D. Tagg; Dr. Kenneth Werrell; Norman Polmar; Filip Zoubek; Evan "Buzz" Nau; Lawrence Paterson; Jim Bauer; Manuela Vittorelli; Dr. Wagner of the Austrian Federal Ministry of the Interior; Major Wade Markel; Justo Miranda; Takeo De Meter; Sergey V. Andreev; Chrins Lee; Ben Evans; Steve Alvin; Jonathan D. Beard; Jason

J. Wehrman; Al Blue; Marcus Hanke; Michael Hyde; Elliot Brown; Casimiro Barreto; Robert Kirchubel; Ann Hassinger; Todd Jahnke; Albert Rosselli; and Richard Benavides.

A special thanks to my editor Heather Ruland Staines for her patience and support, my wife Kathleen for her endless hours of help, and my daughters Olivia and Alexandra for their understanding of my absences from too many family functions while I researched and wrote this book.

# INTRODUCTION

I BEGAN RESEARCHING THIS BOOK OVER A DECADE AGO. MY INTENTION was to write a book substantially different from the one you are presently reading. The work had drawn me into the incredible world of Nazi technology, and what it might have meant for the United States if the war had lasted just a little longer. It was a world populated by scientists and engineers working feverishly to invent new weapons of destruction that might save Nazi Germany from the fate it deserved, or extend its reach across the globe.

They worked on bombers that could fly thousands of miles without stopping to refuel; missiles that could be launched from Europe, reach high into the upper atmosphere of the earth, and in thirty-five minutes come hurtling back down at an unheard-of speed to crash and explode in New York City; rockets that could be catapulted from submarines and travel hundreds of miles to their targets; and a host of other new and deadly weapons. I was concentrating on the weapons and the men who were developing them.

My focus changed in September 1999 when political commentator and presidential candidate Patrick J. Buchanan published a book titled *A Republic, Not an Empire*. The book immediately drew a hailstorm of fire as Buchanan's detractors, and even some friends, focused on two sentences that appeared to challenge the belief that America's participation in World War II had been the "Good War" we have all been led to believe.

The sentences that drew such condemnation were: "If Goering's Luftwaffe could not achieve air supremacy of the [English] Channel, how was it to achieve it over the Atlantic? If Hitler could not put a soldier in England in the fall of 1940, the notion that he could invade the Western Hemisphere—with no surface ships to engage the United States and British fleets and the U.S. airpower dominant in the West Atlantic—was preposterous."[1]

When Buchanan wrote these words he was discussing the United States' entry into war with Germany. His thesis was that President Roosevelt had committed illegal acts by encouraging the U.S. Navy to engage in hostile actions against the German Navy prior to Pearl Harbor. His position was that Germany presented no credible danger to the United States at the time.

As reviewers and newspaper and magazine articles attacked Buchanan over those questions, I wondered just how preposterous it was. I knew from my own work that at least some of the weapons the Germans were developing were especially for targeting the United States. That focused my thinking on Hitler and the role he played in preparing for war against the United States. His fingerprints are extremely difficult to find, because it was his habit to rarely put anything in writing. Even the most important issues were usually dealt with by verbal orders.

The publication of Buchanan's book, and the resulting controversy sparked by charges that he was wrong, and that Hitler was planning an attack on the United States, altered my own research. Some critics charged that Buchanan was underestimating Hitler's intentions toward the United States. Many pointed to reports of an "America Bomber" the Germans were building. Some said Junkers, or Messerschmitt, or Heinkel, depending on the writer, had been manufacturing it. But they were all sure of one thing; Hitler was going to attack the United States mainland at the first opportunity. There were even hints that he had a plan to do this. Sometimes rumor of the plan included an invasion of Brazil for use as a base from which to launch an attack. Others said he wanted to capture the Azores in the mid-Atlantic, and send fleets of heavy bombers over American cities from these Portuguese islands. In the end, though, it was fairly obvious that none of them really knew what Hitler had in mind. But, I began to wonder, were they correct?

Military historians have debated the question of Hitler's intentions toward the United States since the war ended. The issue is clouded by the fact that many Germans denied the United States was a target once they themselves had fallen into Allied hands and were looking for the best deal possible. After all, why admit you were developing a weapon capable of attacking the United States if you hoped to convince the Americans to let you live in their country? A good example of this might be the rocket scientist Werner von Braun. Von Braun always insisted his development of the V-2 missile was for the long-range goal of space exploration, something he helped to accomplish after joining the American space program. He denied he had ever given thought to launching his missiles against the United States, and yet, as you will see in the following pages, we have a very credible report from a slave laborer who claimed he clearly heard von Braun tell a Nazi official that the rocket he was developing would be able to fly across the Atlantic and bomb the United States. Another German official whose reputation was sanitized and who denied any knowledge of a Nazi plan to attack the United States was Armaments Minister Albert Speer. In truth, during the postwar period, no German wanted to be held responsible for a plan, real or imagined, to attack the United States.

Was there a plan to attack America? If so, how close to fruition did the plan progress? To find the answers, I started my search with the one man in Nazi Germany who really mattered, Adolf Hitler. Very little of consequence happened in that country unless Hitler decreed it. He was Nazi Germany! To find the truth, the first questions that must be answered are: What did Hitler think of the United States? Did he anticipate that Germany would have to fight America at some time in the near future? If he did, what preparations did he make for such a conflict? Did he have a plan to attack the United States? How close did he come to launching a successful attack on the United States? The following chapters are the results of my search for the answers to these questions.

The thought of German bombers attacking U.S. targets, or missiles fired at coastal cities from U-boats, was not far-fetched to some American officials during the war. In early 1945 the mayor of New York City ordered a blackout when he feared that Nazi submarines capable of launching rockets at the city had penetrated our naval defenses. *The New York Times* reported that the U.S. Army and Navy had "jointly stated that attacks on this country by V-1 or V-2 bombs are 'entirely possible.' It was assumed the bombs would be launched not from Europe but from submarines lying off our shore, from long-range planes that would make a one-way 'sacrifice flight' and that would be controlled across the Atlantic by submarines or catapult plane tenders."[2]

The danger of German ships equipped with catapults launching bombers against North American targets had been discussed in a 1938 article in *Canadian Defence Quarterly*. Written by Flight Lieutenant A. Carter, and titled "It Can Be Done," the article suggested that "Ships laden with aircraft, equipment, fuel and bombs could enter the Hudson Bay via the North Atlantic and the Hudson Strait, anchor off Churchill or Port Nelson and from this floating base assemble long range bombers which would necessarily have to be float planes or flying boats."[3] Flight Lieutenant Carter appears to have known what he was talking about, for

Germany already had catapult ships and float plane bombers that could easily have made the 625-mile trip to Winnipeg, bombed that city, and returned to their shipboard base. The German airline Deutschlufthansa had for several years been operating a transatlantic service using BV 139 four-engine float planes that made a midocean stop in the Azores and were returned aloft by a catapult ship stationed at the Portuguese islands.

Even before the United States entered the war, a plan was developed to land U.S. marines on the Azores to prevent Hitler from turning the islands into refueling stops for bombers flying west across the Atlantic to North American targets. During the war the expectation that Germany was building long-range bombers capable of transatlantic flights, and missiles aimed at the United States, sometimes influenced the selection of targets for Allied bombing raids in hopes of destroying the factories that were building these weapons. In one case, the Allies created an entirely new weapon based on the belief that German scientists not only had developed a missile that could fly at super speeds across the Atlantic Ocean, but that they had already programmed a track across the great circle route to New York City. According to a U.S. Navy report, the missile that could accomplish the deed would have been ready in the first few months of 1946.

How realistic were these fears of German bomber and missile attacks? It is easy now for us to look back and regard them as a fantasy because the attacks never materialized.

We will examine in detail a plan developed in early 1942 for Hitler, based on his desire to use the Azores as a base from which to attack the United States. The plan includes a list of potential targets, many of which were factories manufacturing aircraft engines, bombsights, and other items critical to our war effort. The author of the plan was a colonel, an engineer, and a specialist in weapons systems and their use. This plan was believed lost at the end of the war. It has never been published and examined in detail before. We will look at the possibility that this plan of attack on the United States, and several other countries, could have been carried out. We will also review the development of the weapons that were required for the plan's success. In the end, we will answer the question: "How close did Nazi Germany come to launching a meaningful attack on the United States?" The answer will surprise many readers.

# CHAPTER 1

# Before There Was a Hitler

*[A] landing on and occupation of Long Island with a resulting threat
to New York from the west end of this island seems feasible.*
VICE ADMIRAL WILHELM BUCHSEL, 1903[1]

IN ORDER TO BETTER UNDERSTAND THE ANIMOSITY HITLER AND THE
Nazis had toward the United States, and Hitler's feelings concerning a
future war against America, it is important that we go back to a time
before there was a Hitler or a Nazi Party. We need to know what the German leaders of the past thought of the United States, and determine if the
hatred the Nazis had toward the American democracy was rooted in the
German governmental psyche.

## WINTERARBEITEN

German military planners first began thinking seriously about the United
States as a potential military target in 1897. Adolf Hitler was eight years
old. They didn't stop thinking about it until the middle of 1945. Winter-
arbeiten were theoretical studies intended to examine the condition of the
military forces of Germany's potential enemies. If war broke out, these
studies would serve as the basis for more in-depth tactical operational
war plans. They were prepared by promising young officers of the German
Navy, and presented to the Kaiser by the chief of the Admiralty Staff.

Prior to 1897 these studies focused primarily on the Imperial German Navy's principal rival, the British Royal Navy. A radical sea change

occurred that year. The first substantive topics involving the United States were assigned to the officers preparing the studies. Topics included questions concerning the Monroe Doctrine, the security of Central America, and the vulnerability of the U.S. mainland. The following year the assignments contained questions regarding a naval bombardment of New York City, and possible landing sites on Long Island and along the Chesapeake Bay.[2]

German naval planners were not the only ones considering the possibility of a German attack against the United States at the time. So was Theodore Roosevelt, Assistant Secretary of the U.S. Navy. On August 11, 1897, in a letter to a member of the British Delegation in Berlin, and a personal friend, Cecil Spring Rice, he wrote that he advocated "keeping our navy at a pitch that will enable us to interfere promptly if Germany ventures to touch a foot of American soil."[3]

German targeting of the United States escalated in the 1899 Winterarbeiten. Prepared under the direction of the future naval historian Lieutenant Eberhard von Mantey, this study more aggressively dealt with an invasion of the United States. Mantey's plans were influenced by reports from Captain Count G. Adolf von Gotzen, Germany's Military Attaché in Washington.

The von Gotzen reports included detailed descriptions of the two military forts protecting the entrance to New York Harbor: Fort Hamilton and Fort Tompkins. Mantey saw New York as his primary target. His war contingency plan called for a surprise attack in which two large naval units would blockade access to the city's harbors. One would be posted at the eastern end of Long Island Sound, sealing off the sound from the Atlantic Ocean between New London, Connecticut, and Orient Point on Long Island's North Fork. The second and more substantial naval force would enter New York's Lower Bay, attack the forts, and shell lower Manhattan.

Meanwhile, several battalions of German infantry and one battalion of engineers would land on Long Island with orders to launch a ground assault on Manhattan the following day. Mantey recognized that a protracted conflict over the occupation of New York City would work against the invaders, placing them far from their supply source. He urged that the invasion be pursued "with the greatest possible energy in order to conclude it in the shortest possible time." If all failed, the troops and ships could fall back onto Block Island, a position from which they could contact Germany for reinforcements.[4]

During the 1920s an ambitious young German naval officer studied these plans for an attack and invasion of New York City. He almost certainly recalled them in early December 1941 as his Fuhrer prepared to declare war against the United States. That officer was Karl Donitz, who as commander of Hitler's U-boat fleets was the first to strike a blow against America. In January 1943 Donitz became Commander-in-Chief of the German Navy. He ultimately succeeded Hitler as Fuhrer of the Third Reich.[5]

An interesting footnote to this particular war plan is that, according to historian Holger H. Herwig, Mantey's father, who was a German Army general, wrote two letters to his son urging him to focus his plan on an "attack against the United States" because it was a subject of such topical interest that it was sure to find its way to the upper reaches of the German Admiralty. General Mantey was correct.[6]

One of the more fascinating responses to Mantey's 1899 Winter-arbeiten for an invasion of New York City came from Vice Admiral August Thomsen, commander of the First Battle Squadron, and Germany's highest-ranking active duty commanding officer. Thomsen believed that the weakest link in Mantey's plan was the need to steam across the Atlantic and launch a surprise attack. He expected that American intelligence agents would detect such a large war fleet traveling the required distance. Thomsen's suggested alternative is of special interest because a variation was reintroduced during the Second World War. The admiral proposed that the fleet attack Puerto Rico and occupy that island, forcing the U.S. Navy to either defend the island, or launch a counterattack. It would also position the U.S. Navy at a distance from its own supply bases. Puerto Rico could then be used as a launching pad for attacks on the U.S. mainland, and an invasion by German infantry. Although he conceded ignorance of how the U.S. government would react to such an invasion, Thomsen believed "that much will have been accomplished when we have taken and hold the American northeast."[7]

In the years following Mantey's plan, Germany never lost sight of the United States as a target. In 1900 the situation evolved into a Marschplan (plan of advance) that called for an armada of German warships crossing the Atlantic, with a stop in the Azores for coal, then on to the United States. This time the targets were New York and Boston. To support the plan, the German naval attaché in Washington was ordered to reconnoiter acceptable landing sites along the coast between those two cities. Also in support of the plan, the Reichstag approved a Naval Bill providing the funds for a fleet of thirty-eight battleships, twenty large cruisers, and thirty-eight light cruisers.

In 1901 the Kaiser himself proposed an invasion of Cuba. His reasoning was that it could be used as a base from which to launch an attack on the United States. Building a new, more powerful navy that could be used successfully against the United States, which had a few years earlier demonstrated its own strength against Spain in the Spanish-American War, was not going to be accomplished overnight, so the planners continued to examine their options. They also attempted to determine how America would respond to an invasion of New York and Boston, and the numbers of troops that could be thrown against the invaders. Both army and navy leaders agreed that Cape Cod would serve as "a base for operations against Boston as well as against New York."8

On March 21, 1903, the head of the German Admiralty, Vice Admiral Wilhelm Buchsel, told the Kaiser: "There can be only one objective for Germany's war strategy: direct pressure on the American East Coast and its most populous areas, especially New York. That is, a merciless offensive designed to confront the American people with an unbearable situation through the dissemination of terror and through damaging enemy trade and property." There was now "little doubt among Germany's political as well as military leaders that the United States had become the most probable future opponent."9

For the next three years, until political alignments in Europe turned to Germany's disadvantage, her military planners worked to refine what was called Operation Plan III, war against the United States. Various schemes were examined, including direct attacks and the forced occupation of several Caribbean islands to use as bases. In the end it became abundantly clear that Germany would not in the foreseeable future be powerful enough to defeat the U.S. Navy at sea and invade the U.S. mainland. Besides, her land forces were soon locked in a deadly two-front war across the European continent.

## CONFRONTATION AT MANILA

In the midst of all this war planning by the Germans, a real war broke out. On February 15, 1898, the U.S. Navy's battleship *Maine* was wracked by a series of explosions and was sunk with great loss of life in the harbor at Havana, Cuba. Cuba at the time was a much-abused colony of Spain. The United States, at the behest of important expansionists such as Assistant Navy Secretary Theodore Roosevelt, had been pressing Spain to withdraw from Cuba and give the island its independence. The war that resulted from the destruction of the *Maine* was not between Germany and the United States, but the United States and the gradually decaying Spanish empire.

The Spanish-American War was fought in two theaters, Cuba and the Philippines. The U.S. Asiatic Fleet, under command of Commodore George Dewey, surprised the Spanish fleet at Manila and bottled it up by blockading the entrance to Manila Bay after bombarding the Spanish ships on May 1, 1898. Dewey was unable to force a Spanish surrender because he lacked enough troops to land and engage the twenty thousand Spanish soldiers stationed in Manila. He waited for the promised arrival of the troops required to complete his mission.

On May 6, a German Navy warship, the cruiser *Irene*, arrived on the scene. She ignored signals from the blockading American fleet to stop, steamed into Manila Bay, and dropped anchor. Three days later she was joined by another German warship, the cruiser *Cormoran*. This second cruiser also ignored signals from the American vessels to stop. Fearing that the Germans were going to get into the war on the Spanish side, Dewey decided to show them he meant business. The *Cormoran* halted only after one of Dewey's gunboats fired a shot across her bow. Dewey was wrong: Germany wasn't interested in joining the war on Spain's side—she, in the person of the Kaiser's brother Prince Henry, was attempting to find a way to alter the Philippines' position as a Spanish colony to a German colony. To that end the Germans flaunted international protocol when a blockading fleet is in place, and landed a small number of German troops.

On June 12 another German cruiser, the *Kaiserin Augusta,* flagship of Vice Admiral von Diedrichs, arrived. Another cruiser and a transport carrying fourteen hundred men quickly followed. Dewey grew concerned over the arrival of so many German warships, especially since two of them were of larger displacement than any ship in his own fleet. It began to appear as if the Germans, whose officers regularly landed in the city and were warmly greeted by the Spanish, were preparing to force the Americans to back down and move away from Manila Bay.[10]

Meanwhile, in Berlin, the German Foreign Office attempted to use the presence of the German warships in Manila Bay as leverage to force the American ambassador, Andrew D. White, to agree to grant the German Navy concessions in the form of naval bases in the Philippines. The U.S. Naval Attaché in the German capital, Commander Francis Barber, urged Washington toward "immediately doubling Dewey's squadron."[11]

At Manila Bay a brief meeting between von Diedrichs and Dewey did not go well. Neither man was going to be pushed around by the other. Dewey saw the Germans as interlopers who presented a potential danger to his squadron. Von Diedrichs was of the opinion that it would be a "long, long time" before the United States would constitute "a respectable" military power. The possibility of even a minor incident exploding into a major battle between the German and American fleets hung heavily in the air.[12]

Germany and the United States stepped back from their naval confrontation when the Spanish forces at Manila surrendered to Dewey and the U.S. Army troops he had finally been able to put ashore.[13]

## THE GREAT WAR INVASION PLAN

World War I offered German military planners a renewed opportunity to consider the United States a target for attack. Before America's entry into the war, German and Allied agents operated across the nation, purchasing war goods for their respective sides, and attempting to influence American public opinion.

Despite German plans for building a world-class navy, Great Britain and her allies maintained control of the Atlantic Ocean for all of World War I. As the war dragged on, the Germans found it exceedingly difficult to safely ship their purchases from America to Europe. This gave rise to renewed efforts by German agents in the propaganda arena. Their goal became one of shoring up support for President Wilson's neutrality policy. Since they were unable to make use of war material they were buying here, they hoped to stop the sale of such items to their opponents. They had some minor success when several labor unions under the influence of German agents went on strike against companies producing goods for the British.

President Wilson was concerned about violations of the neutrality policy. He asked Treasury Secretary William McAdoo to take all appropriate steps to stop any violations by representatives of either side. As a result, the U.S. Secret Service began keeping a close watch on known agents, recording their comings and goings and with whom they met.

Among those being tailed by Secret Service agents was George Sylvester Viereck, suspected of being a German propaganda agent. On July 24, 1915, with two agents following him, Viereck entered a building on New York's Lower Broadway. The building housed the offices of the Hamburg-American Steamship Company. The two agents, Frank Burke and William Houghton, waited patiently for Viereck to exit the building. When he finally did, a second man whom the agents did not know accompanied him. The man was later identified as Dr. Heinrich Albert, Commercial Attaché of the German Embassy in Washington.

With the two Secret Service agents close behind, Viereck and Albert walked to the Sixth Avenue elevated train station and boarded a train heading uptown. While the Germans sat quietly speaking in low voices, Burke and Houghton kept a watchful eye on them. They were both aware that the second man, as yet unknown to them, was holding his briefcase unusually securely against his body.

When the train stopped at the 23rd Street station, Viereck said goodbye to his companion and left the train. Agent Houghton also departed the train and followed Viereck. Albert, perhaps relaxing slightly, put the briefcase down on the seat Viereck had just vacated, and began reading a newspaper.

The train continued its journey north, stopping at several stations. At the 50th Street station, Albert, who had evidently been so engrossed in his newspaper that he didn't notice the train was stopped at his station, suddenly looked up and shouted "Wait" to the conductor, who was preparing to close the doors. Still holding his newspaper, Albert jumped from his seat and rushed out the door. Once on the platform he realized he had forgotten his briefcase, but when he rushed back into the car a woman passenger seated nearby indicated another man had taken it and fled out another door. Albert gave chase to the man, who was none other than Secret Service Agent Frank Burke.

Burke had watched as Albert left the train without his briefcase, and on impulse Burke grabbed it and ran. With the frantic German in hot pursuit he bolted down the stairs to the sidewalk and leapt aboard a passing streetcar. A few blocks away he left the streetcar and headed for the Secret Service's New York offices. The head of the service, William J. Flynn, who happened by chance to be in New York that day, joined him.

Together, Flynn and Burke opened the briefcase. It was packed with documents. Unfortunately, they were all written in German, a language neither agent knew, but the men quickly realized that these documents were probably important. They were right. When Secretary McAdoo had the documents translated, they revealed that Albert, along with the German Military Attaché Captain Franz von Papen, were distributing up to $2 million each week in support of German espionage and propaganda operations in the United States. It was all laid out—union officials who had been bribed to call strikes, and plans to gain control of an American aircraft manufacturer, and to corner the market on the production of liquid chlorine, which was used in making poison gas.

Perhaps most shocking of all to American officials, the briefcase also contained the plans for a German invasion of the United States. In these plans, over one hundred thousand German soldiers were to come ashore along the virtually unprotected and unguarded New Jersey beachfront in two succeeding waves. These troops were to rush northward and attempt to seal off New York City from the mainland. The developers of the plan estimated that New York contained less than a week's supply of food, and that following this period the American government would be willing to negotiate surrender terms rather than see thousands starve to death in the city. As in many of the plans the Germans worked on before and after, they always underestimated the will of the American people to fight back against an aggressor.

Also discovered in Dr. Albert's briefcase was the key to a secret German code. The information it provided enabled American agents to decipher the infamous Zimmermann telegram, in which a German Foreign Office official proposed to the Mexican government a joint German-Mexican invasion of the southwestern United States and the return to Mexico of those territories lost years earlier to the United States. After the war, Viereck compared losing the briefcase to the loss of the USS *Maine* at the start of the Spanish-American War.[14]

World War I brought with it an entirely new potential danger to the United States from Germany: bombing from the air. The possibility first appeared publicly in an article in the *London Observer* newspaper in late 1917. Without identifying its sources, the article inferred that the Germans might attempt such an attack the following year. One American official who took the threat seriously was Admiral Robert E. Peary, who was concerned with air defense issues. Peary told reporters he considered a German air raid against New York City a "distinct possibility."

The threat was not that the enemy had an airplane capable of flying across the ocean and bombing New York City—that was decades away—but that a bomber floatplane could be dismantled and packed into one of the deadly German submarines, which could transport it to a location off the East Coast. Once situated, the sub could capture a freighter and use its cargo-handling equipment to move the crated aircraft onto the ship's deck and reassemble it for its mission. The arrival of German U-boats off Long Island a few months later gave some credibility to the story. Luckily, the Germans never appeared to actually think of this themselves, at least not during that war.[15]

Judging by this history, we can see that long before Hitler became Chancellor, even long before he became a would-be artist, German military leaders, including the Kaiser, viewed the United States of America as an enemy, and sought ways in which to attack her. What followed during the Nazi period was little more than an extension of the same policies and the same desire to strike at the world's foremost democracy.

## CHAPTER 2

# Adolf Hitler, America, and the World

*"I don't see much future for the Americans. In my view it's a decayed country."*

ADOLF HITLER, 1/7/42[1]

THE GERMAN GOVERNMENT'S VIEW OF THE UNITED STATES DURING THE rule of Hitler and the Nazis was so badly mistaken that it led, ultimately, to their downfall. In a sense, Germany had no opinion of the United States that was not Hitler's. As noted historian Gerhard L. Weinberg has pointed out, when policy formulation is restricted to one man, then his perception is the significant factor in that nation's international relations. The defect in Germany's ability to understand and evaluate the United States as a potential enemy was rooted in Hitler's understanding, or lack of understanding, of the United States. As for Hitler, his view of the United States and much of the world beyond Germany changed little. Hitler "was little affected by experience which leads other men to adjust erroneous perceptions to facts."[2]

What change there was in Hitler's opinion of the United States came about shortly before he achieved power. It never changed after that, despite the "facts" demonstrating that he was underestimating his most powerful adversary. Interestingly, his original opinion of the United States was correct. During the 1920s Hitler viewed America as Europe's greatest future rival, a sort of sleeping giant that one day "would strive for world domination."[3]

## A PRODUCT OF THE GREAT WAR

Adolf Hitler, and a great many other Germans, could never reconcile themselves with the reality that Germany had lost the First World War. Like many conspiracy advocates who can't accept the truth, they subscribed to a fabricated theory that explained what was to them unexplainable. Germany had not lost the war on the battlefields of western Europe. The German Army was not beaten by the combined strength of the Allied armies. Germany, according to its theory, was beaten not from the front, but from the rear in what was to become known as the "stab in the back." The failure was not with the military leadership of the German Army, but with the cowardice and treachery of politicians, especially those who had signed the Treaty of Versailles ending the war.

Of course the reality was different. During the first half of 1918 the German Army successfully pursued the war, driving the Allies back almost into Paris itself. German troops were less than forty miles from the French capital when the whole world appeared to collapse for the German people. In the words of Hitler biographer Alan Bullock, "The situation of the German Army by November 1918 was in fact without hope. It was only a matter of time before it was driven back into Germany and destroyed."[4]

The reality was that the final Allied offensive that began in August 1918 had broken the back of the German Army. In one hundred days the Allies took 363,000 German prisoners, fully one quarter of the German Army then in the field, and captured 6,400 guns. The latter represented one half of the German Army's artillery.[5]

The truth of this situation was withheld from the German civilian population by the army's leadership. They were led to believe that it was a combination of communist revolutionaries and traitorous politicians who had decided to end the war in defeat while the army was on the verge of victory. It was on this lie that numerous German nationalist groups, including the Nazis, fed and grew.

For the most part the Allied leaders were ignorant of the dangerous situation they were helping to create in Germany by permitting this lie to be born. One who wasn't was the commander of the American

Expeditionary Force, General John J. Pershing. On learning that the armistice terms had been agreed to, Pershing commented: "What I dread is that Germany doesn't know that she has been licked. Had they given us another week, we'd have taught them."[6]

The seed of Nazism was planted deep within this lie that had been invented by German generals unable to face the humiliation of their own defeat. It also gave rise to the myth of the indestructible German Army, and failed to recognize the superiority of the Allied forces, both in numbers and in weaponry. It would take a second war for that truth to enter the German consciousness. The lie blinded Germans to the growing power of the nation they knew little about, the United States. The lie allowed them to believe that American entry into the war had little impact on its outcome, because that outcome had been decided not at the front, but behind the army's back.

Adolf Hitler not only fed on this lie, but he actually believed it. And because he believed it, he failed to understand the significance of the United States' entry into the war. That failure led him to underestimate the ability of the United States to mobilize and fight a massive war against two enemies on two separate fronts at the same time. The failure to realize the importance to the Allied victory of American participation in the last war lead inevitably to an underestimation of what the impact of American participation in the new war would be on German plans for conquest.

## UNDERESTIMATING AMERICA

America's enemies have habitually underestimated her. During the eighteenth century, King George III miscalculated the will and resilience of the population of the American colonies to withstand the onslaught of the world's mightiest professional army and navy. As a result, the British crown lost the most valuable jewel it possessed.

Near the end of the nineteenth century, as Spain and the United States moved toward war over the independence of Cuba, Spanish officials thought it humorous that the United States dared to challenge the Spanish Empire's claims of sovereignty in the Americas. The April 6, 1898, edition of a leading Madrid newspaper quoted a Spanish naval official who claimed that as soon as Spanish warships opened fire on American warships, "the crews of the American ships will commence to desert, since we all know that among them are people of all nationalities."[7]

The Spanish changed their attitude once American naval and land forces soundly defeated them in Cuba and the Philippines.

The view that the United States was a weakened nation as a result of the diversity of the racial makeup of her population would surface again among Nazi leaders four decades later. In his social history of Nazi Germany, Richard Grunberger described the German view of the United States as "a polyglot, mongrelized community descended from convicts and the unwanted dregs of other societies."[8]

Alan Bullock claims one of the reasons Hitler rushed to declare war on the United States right after the Japanese attack on Pearl Harbor, and while the German Army was struggling against a very effective Soviet counterattack, was that "[t]he mixture of races in its population, as well as the freedom and lack of authoritarian discipline in its life, predisposed him to regard it as another decadent bourgeois democracy, incapable of any sustained military effort."[9]

A more recent adversary who underestimated the American people and then paid severely for it was the Islamic terrorist leader Osama bin Laden. He evidently thought we would cower as a result of a violent attack on civilian targets. He and his entire international terrorist network learned differently.

What these enemies failed to recognize was that a powerful new American culture and society had been built on the absorption of so many people from so many different places.

## HITLER'S VIEW OF THE UNITED STATES

During his lifetime, Adolf Hitler wrote two books filled with his views and ideas. The first, and most successful and mostly widely translated of these, was *Mein Kampf*, which translates to "My Struggle." It became the bible of the Nazi Party. Hitler's original title for the book was "Four and a Half Years of Struggle Against Lies, Stupidity, and Cowardice," but his Nazi Party publisher Max Amann prevailed on him to shorten it. Amann believed the more succinct title would help increase its sales. Dictated mostly while he was in a rather comfortable prison environment following the failed beer hall putsch of 1923, the book was published in two volumes. The first volume was published in the autumn of 1925, and the second in the summer of 1926. Although at first these books, which run to nearly eight hundred pages combined, sold poorly, Hitler's rise to power changed that. During his rule of Germany, municipal governments were required to present copies to newlyweds as gifts. It was also typically given to schoolchildren on their graduation.[10]

Although there is little reference to the United States in *Mein Kampf*, in his next book, written in 1928 but not published until 1961 under the title *Hitlers Zweites Buch* ("Hitler's Second Book"), he dealt with the United States. It was here that he predicted a future war with the United States. His earlier book made it obvious that to achieve his goals of expanding the German nation, Germany would have to engage in two wars. One war would be against France to regain the industrial areas lost to France through the Treaty of Versailles; the second, against the Soviet Union to gain additional agricultural territory on which to raise the crops to feed a mighty new nation. In his view, the United States represented a "real threat to German domination of the world." A third war would be required to deal with this peril, one in which only a united Europe ruled or dominated by Germany could be successful. "One of the major tasks of the National Socialists (Nazis) would be the preparation of Germany for this conflict."[11]

By the early 1930s, Hitler's opinion of the United States had changed. America was no longer the potentially powerful rival he had earlier envisioned. According to Gerhard L. Weinberg, one reason for this change in attitude toward the United States was the impact on that nation of the Great Depression. Hitler thought the effects of the worldwide financial collapse on the United States were permanent. Because of this, "Hitler concluded that the United States was really a very weak country."[12]

In addition, he came under the influence of crackpot geopolitical theorists who themselves failed to comprehend the inherent strength of this radically different, yet potentially cohesive society. As a result, Hitler all but ignored the giant across the Atlantic. Throughout the rest of his life, even as American troops overran his mighty Third Reich, Hitler's disdain toward America never changed. It was a society "half Judaised, the other half negrified. How can one expect a state like that to hold together?"13

America, Hitler claimed, and most likely believed since he was apparently blinded by his own hatreds, was without the cultural foundations required of a civilized society. In a moment of high hubris he declared, "[O]ne Beethoven symphony contains more culture than America has produced in her whole history."14

Throughout the 1930s and the 1940s, this perception of the United States as a degraded culture ruled over by the hated Jews prevailed as not only what Hitler personally believed, but also the official image provided to the German people by their government. Historian Holger H. Herwig describes a so-called documentary film produced by propaganda minister Josef Goebbels in November 1941, one month before Hitler declared war on the United States. The film was titled *A Stroll Through America*. Running fifteen minutes and made for viewing in movie theaters throughout Germany, the film purports to show President Roosevelt and his "Jewish henchmen" addressing the U.S. Congress. There are reports of strikes "suppressed brutally with gun and gas," and shots of slum housing, hunger strikes, "grotesque Negro dances," and lurid news reports of suicides.15

The sycophants who were appointed to important posts reinforced Hitler's opinion of the United States. For many of them the truth was less important than pleasing the Fuhrer. David Kahn provides us with a wonderful example of one of these men who, had he had the courage and honesty required of his post, might have altered the way in which Hitler treated the possibility of American entry into the war. General Friedrich von Boetticher was the German military attaché in Washington. Boetticher appears to have never let reality interfere with his dispatches to Berlin, which were constantly colored by his belief that America was under the control of the "Jewish element."

Boetticher ignored all the signs that might give pause to an open-minded military attaché, including the vast industrial might of the United States and the millions of military-aged men available to the government should war come. Instead, he focused on supporting his belief that should the United States enter the war, it would look to Japan as the most dangerous enemy to be dealt with first, and the United States would not concern herself with Europe until it was too late to alter a German victory. According to Kahn, in September 1940, he reported that finding a military or political solution to the situation in the Pacific Ocean was "the first aim of the United States." He repeated this theme in July 1941 and again in November. He even chose to ignore the importance of a report published in the *Chicago Tribune* and the *Washington Times-Herald* on December 4, 1941, that the defeat of Germany would be the "first major objective of the United States" if she entered the war. Kahn claims that despite the disastrous nature of the information supplied by Boetticher, "Hitler read it, liked it, and acted upon it."[16]

There is some irony to the fact that Hitler evidently made important decisions based on Boetticher's dispatches primarily because they supported his own view of the United States. Yet, William L. Shirer reports that two officers of the Army High Command told him that the General Staff was "highly suspicious of the objectivity of the reports from the Washington embassy," and had established a separate source for military intelligence in the United States.[17]

Of course, not all Germans saw the Americans, especially American troops, through the distorted Nazi lens. This was especially true of the men who faced those troops on the battlefield. Typical of many of these was General Baron Rudolf von Gersdorf's opinion of U.S. soldiers during the 1944 Ardennes campaign: "The American soldier proved himself once again to be a very worthy, well-trained and physically tough opponent."[18]

## FUHRER OF THE WORLD

While Hitler was not a great long-term thinker and strategist, there can be little doubt that somewhere in the back of that mad mind was the desire to rule the world. Others have had the same desire with even less to work with, so why not Hitler? His concept of how he saw his role in the world can be seen as early as 1927, in a letter written by his closest advisor and confidant, Rudolf Hess. The letter was addressed to another close Nazi supporter, Walter Hewel, who was living in London at the time. Hess wrote, ". . . in Hitler's opinion it [world peace] will be realizable only when one power, the racially best power, has attained complete and uncontested supremacy. That [power] can then provide a sort of world police" that will ensure the "most valuable race" has all the space it requires, and keep the "lower races" from breeding too much.[19]

A simple overview of how he conducted his war puts to rest the claims of some historians that because Hitler was a "continental man," he had no plans for the world beyond Europe. While there may not have been an actual plan, there is certain logic to the steps of conquest he followed. First, Austria, Czechoslovakia, and Poland, giving him some elbow room to his east. Then France, the Low Countries, Denmark, and Norway give him control over territory to his west. This is followed by a forced settlement with Great Britain in which the British align themselves with the German-dominated Europe. Next comes a sweep across Russia to the Ural Mountains, something that almost everyone in the West, with the possible exception of President Roosevelt, believed he would accomplish in a few short months. If the British had thrown in the towel and the Soviets had collapsed, what next?

By the summer of 1941 a lot of people thought they knew what was next, even those in the United States, far removed from the action. A *Fortune* poll "found that 72 percent of the respondents felt that Hitler would not be satisfied until he had tried to conquer everything, including the Americas."[20]

We are given a hint of what was next in July 1941. While Britain failed to capitulate, Hitler remained confident of final victory on that front. In the east his forces, supported by allied armies from other central European nations, continued to sweep across Russia toward ultimate victory. With success virtually assured, the Germans began what Gerhard L. Weinberg called "postwar planning." This "once again included the huge surface fleet. Projected at 25 battleships, 8 aircraft carriers, 50 cruisers, 400 submarines, 150 destroyers, and miscellaneous other ships, it provides important insight into German long-term policy aims toward the Western Hemisphere—unless one is prepared to assume that the big ships were to be sent down the Danube or hauled by rail to the Caspian Sea."[21]

Hitler's long-term goal was to be Fuhrer of the world. The speed with which he declared war on the United States when that step was not necessary, in part because he was enamored with the idea that his decision would impact the lives of millions of people around the world, reveals this clearly. This new war, which now included the Western Hemisphere as well as Asia, "excited Hitler's imagination with its taste for the grandiose and stimulated that sense of historic destiny which was the drug on which he fed."[22]

On December 11, 1941, before a cheering mob of Reichstag deputies, Hitler made his declaration of war against the United States. He told them that this "historic struggle" would in the future be described as "decisive not only for the history of Germany but for the whole of Europe and indeed the world."[23]

Where did the United States fit in his plans? Gerhard L. Weinberg puts it succinctly when he writes that Hitler "decided early on—long before he became Chancellor—to conquer the world. From this he deduced very logically that war with the United States would be necessary since the Americans would not give up their independence because of his good looks. So already in 1928 he maintained that preparing for war with the United States would be one of the main projects of a Nazi government."[24]

## CHAPTER 3

# The Plan to Bomb America

UNTIL RECENTLY, LITTLE WAS KNOWN ABOUT HITLER'S LONG-RANGE bombing and transportation plan. Many military historians and researchers doubted the very existence of an actual plan for a transoceanic bombing campaign. Those who believed the plan existed assumed it had been destroyed or lost as the war came to a close. Not until its discovery in the Military Archives at Potsdam by German historian Olaf Groehler could the world know what Hitler's Luftwaffe was hoping to accomplish beyond the European continental limits.

Noted historian Holger H. Herwig suggests that the plan was the result of discussions by Hitler in November 1940 and again in May 1941 of his desire to "deploy long-range bombers against American cities from the Azores." Because Germany did not have a bomber capable of making the round-trip from Europe to America and back without a refueling stop, Hitler saw the Azores as his "only possibility of carrying out aerial attacks from a land base against the United States." In November he ordered a study to determine whether the Azores port and aircraft landing facilities could meet his needs. On May 22, 1941, Hitler returned to the subject of launching bombing raids against American cities, especially from the Azores.[1]

Herwig believes the discovery of the plan "confirms that Hitler had every intention of bringing the war to the United States" after he had conquered the Soviet Union.[2]

The Luftwaffe experts completed work on the plan on April 27, 1942. They submitted it to Reichsmarshal Hermann Göring on May 12, 1942.

The final version of the plan runs thirty-three pages. Attached to it is a map of the world showing various targets and flight patterns. The flight patterns include notations of the types of long-range aircraft to be used for each flight destination. Included within the heart of the plan are schemas of those aircraft.[3]

Ten copies of the document were made. Six were distributed to various Luftwaffe offices, and four were held in reserve. I worked from a photocopy of original copy number five.

## THE MAN WITH THE PLAN

The plan for a long-range bombing campaign against the United States was prepared under the direction of Luftwaffe Colonel-Engineer Dietrich Schwenke. Schwenke oversaw technical intelligence gathering, and reported directly to Field Marshal Erhard Milch, the Luftwaffe's air armaments chief. The colonel operated a test and evaluation center at Rechlin, where captured or downed enemy aircraft were brought to be either dissected for closer examination, or repaired and test-flown by German pilots. During the 1940 invasion of France and Belgium, Schwenke, who had once served as assistant air attaché in London, developed a systemized approach to collecting captured Allied aircraft for shipment to Rechlin. Eventually he employed two hundred selected Russian prisoners of war at Rechlin for the task of dismantling captured enemy airplanes.[4]

Schwenke himself once flew an American B-17, when that bomber was generating the most interest among the Luftwaffe leadership. He reported the huge four-engine bomber to be "extraordinarily easy" to fly. Schwenke was especially impressed by the fact the cockpit was so quiet during flight that the pilot and copilot could converse with each other in normal speaking voices. David Kahn described Schwenke, whom he met and interviewed in 1973, as "a smart, tough pilot with an engineering background and lots of foreign experience."[5]

Schwenke periodically takes center stage at crucial moments throughout the war. During the first week of March 1941 he was sent to Russia to assess the strength of the Soviet Air Force and the capacity of Soviet aircraft production plants. This was three months before the German attack on the Soviet Union. According to Hitler's Luftwaffe adjutant, Nicolaus von Below, Schwenke reported to the Fuhrer that the Soviets were "arming on a grand scale."[6]

Following the especially horrific bombing of the German Baltic port city of Lubeck on March 28, 1942, Schwenke searched the wreckage of a Royal Air Force Wellington bomber and made a vital discovery. He found a navigational aid the British code-named Gee.[7] Invented the year before, Gee allowed British navigators to use radio signals to pinpoint their positions during night bombing raids. Gee had contributed immeasurably to the RAF's successful night bomber campaigns. The discovery quickly led to the German development of technology to successfully jam the Gee signals.[8]

A short time later Schwenke warned the Luftwaffe Chief of Staff General Hans Jeschonnek of the large numbers of four-engine B-17 bombers that the Americans were ferrying across the Atlantic for use against German cities.[9]

Schwenke evidently worked on several important projects, including methods of jamming radar. David Irving credits him with revealing to Field Marshal Milch the British use of metallic foil strips hung from balloons to confuse the German early warning system known as "Freya." He warned Milch that although the British were not using the balloons to a large degree, there was the possibility of greater success of confusing German radar if they expanded the number of balloons they sent toward German territory.[10]

In order to determine the capacity of enemy aircraft manufacturing, which would in turn help predict their future strategy, Schwenke formed a unit at Rechlin for analyzing and deciphering the serial numbers on parts from Allied planes that had been shot down or crashed. It is reported that this unit "provided apparently solid data" on aircraft production by both the Soviets and the Americans, because both used consecutive serial numbering systems. They were less successful with British aircraft production, where the numbers were not as reliably successive.[11]

Schwenke's careful research into the construction of enemy bombers proved especially productive when he was able to show German fighter pilots the exact location of fuel tanks on the different models used by the Americans and British. He was also able to recommend the caliber of ammunition that could most successfully penetrate the bomber's armor and ignite the fuel tanks. In this way he solved the puzzle raised by fighter pilots who reported numerous hits on Allied bombers that failed to bring the aircraft down.[12]

The period from September 1939 to May 1940 on the western front was called the Phony War by the American press. British Prime Minister Neville Chamberlain said it was the "twilight war." During this time all the fighting was taking place in the east, despite the fact that both Britain and France had declared war on Germany on September 3, 1939, over the German invasion of Poland. As German forces were built up for an invasion through Belgium and Holland, the French Army remained behind the much-vaunted Maginot Line, smugly confident that the fixed defenses would prevent the Germans from invading France. Schwenke was instrumental in delaying a planned air attack in the west in September when he reported to Göring his personal sighting of 150 Spitfire fighters ready for action at six different airfields. He predicted that over half an attacking German bomber force would be shot down if the attack took place as planned. Göring passed this information to Hitler, who decided to delay an attack in the west for several months, giving the Luftwaffe a chance to improve its ability to defend its bombers against British fighters.[13]

## "Tasks for Long-Range Aircraft"

The plan itself is comprised of thirty-three pages. Of this total, twenty-two pages are text, and two pages are diagrams indicating the flight range of six different German long-range bomber aircraft. The final nine pages are schematic drawings of the six aircraft mentioned in the diagrams, plus three additional long-range bombers. Attached to all this is a folded map that when opened measures approximately thirteen by twenty-two inches.

Page 1 is a combination of title page and contents page listing each of the individual eight sections into which the plan is divided. Also included on this page is a listing of the distribution of the first six copies of the plan to various high-ranking Luftwaffe officers. There is also a notation that copies numbered seven through ten were held in reserve. At the bottom is the information concerning the number of pages, and that the plan was completed in Berlin on April 27, 1942. At the lower right-hand corner of the page is a signature believed to be that of Dietrich Schwenke. Below the signature is the title "Colonel-Engineer."

At the top of the page the document is addressed to "The Reich Minister of Aviation and the Commander in Chief of the Luftwaffe," who was none other than Hermann Göring himself. The center of the page reads as follows:

### Tasks for Long-Range Aircraft

I. Summary

II. Transportation of scarce resources and their monthly German requirement

III. Air transport connections with Japan and the available type of aircraft and their transport capacity

IV. Long-range aircraft for the year 1942 as well as 1943/44

V. Reconnaissance and military targets in the Soviet Union

VI. Reconnaissance and military targets in the Middle and Northeast Africa and the Persian Gulf

VII. Reconnaissance and military targets on the West Atlantic coast and in the USA

VIII. 1 world map showing the targets, the routes, and the distances[14]

The three-page summary is divided into four subsections. Subsections A through C describe the scarcity of various raw materials and the potential use of long-range transport aircraft. These airplanes would replace blockade-running ships to bring such materials from distant locations such as Finland, Siberia, and Africa. The fourth subsection is key to our discussion. It reads as follows:

**D. West Atlantic Area and USA: Reconnaissance and Bomb Targets.**
On the coast of the USA there are aluminum works, aircraft engine works, propeller works and arms factories; these can only be attacked by Messerschmitt 264 with DB 613 motors carrying 5.5 tons of bombs and starting from Brest. If the Azores could be used as a transit airfield it would be possible to reach these targets with He 177 (refueled) with

*2 tons, BV 222 (refueled) with 4.5 tons, Ju 290 with 5 tons, and Me 264 with 6.5 tons. The Panama Canal cannot be attacked with the planes mentioned, unless there can be a refueling at sea (BV 222).[15]*

Section II, "Transportation of scarce resources and their monthly German requirement," deals with the shortage of raw materials in Germany, the monthly German requirements of those materials, and the opportunity for purchasing them from Japanese-controlled areas in Asia. It also discusses the possibility of using heavy long-range transport aircraft to bring these materials to German-controlled Europe. The raw materials the Germans sought from their Asian allies included tin, rubber, copper, platinum, and tungsten.

This section also mentions that raw materials from Japanese-controlled areas could be traded for medicines and pharmaceuticals produced in Germany. It also recommends that some of these raw materials might be acquired from South American countries. Among the countries discussed are Argentina and Chile, which are referred to as anti-German, and Brazil, Columbia, and Bolivia.

Section III, "Air transport connections with Japan and the available type of aircraft and their transport capacity," concerns the creation of long-range air links between German-occupied Europe and the Japanese-occupied Asian mainland. Included are the estimated air miles from Germany to Manchuria and Malaysia, as well as between Berlin and Nagasaki, Japan.

Included in this section is a chart listing the take-off weight, payload capacities, and flight duration performances of five military aircraft models. They are the He 177; Fw 200; BV 222; Ju 290; and Me 264. A second chart lists similar performance data for four additional military aircraft that were expected to be ready for use during 1943 and 1944. These were the Fw 300; BV 238S; BV 238L; and the Ju 390. All nine aircraft were at the time, or would soon be capable of performing as, long-range reconnaissance, transport, and/or bombers.

Section IV, "Long-range aircraft for the year 1942 as well as 1943/44," contains a brief discussion of the various missions in which these aircraft could be engaged. Two diagrams depicting the payload capacities and the

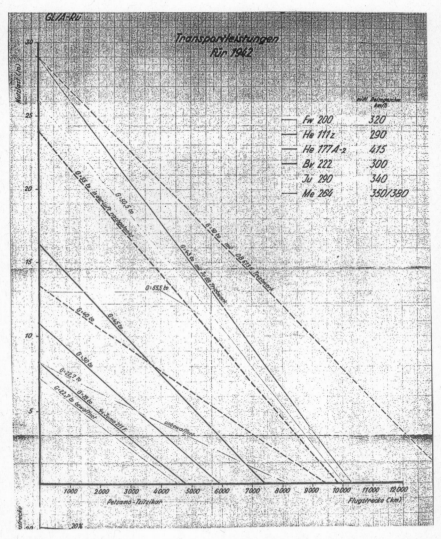

Official German chart showing range and payload capacity of six aircraft available in 1942.

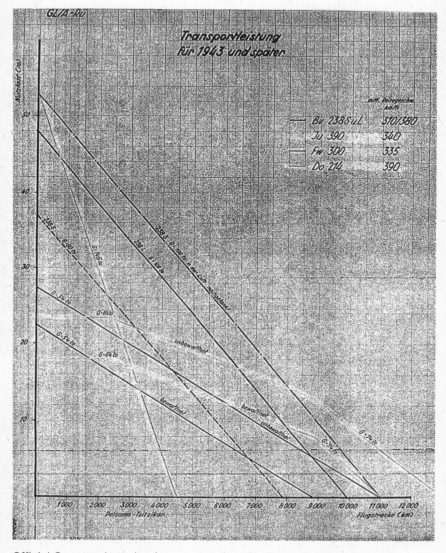

Official German chart showing range and payload capacity of four aircraft expected to be available in 1943 and 1944.

range of these planes follow the text. The first diagram is for aircraft in use or impending use in 1942. The second diagram covers aircraft expected to be in service in 1943 and later. Both diagrams are included in this chapter.

Following the diagrams are nine pages, each containing schematic drawings of the type of long-range aircraft that could be used for the various missions discussed in the plan, including bombing raids on American targets. All nine drawings are included here as well.

Section V, "Reconnaissance and military targets in the Soviet Union," focuses on combat goals that could be achieved by long-range bombers in territory held by the Soviet Union. It includes a listing of target sites and the variety of war work done at those sites. It also provides estimates of the importance of the manufacturing plants at those sites to the Soviet war effort. Among the thirty-four targets listed in Soviet-held territory are the oil production centers at Baku on the Caspian Sea; the aircraft production plants at Irkutsk near the Mongolian border; the central Russian city of Kazan, where synthetic rubber, aircraft engine, and bomb production plants were located; and the munitions, small arms, and artillery manufacturing facilities around the central Russian city of Sverdlovsk.

Section VI, "Reconnaissance and military targets in the Middle and Northeast Africa and the Persian Gulf," includes a list of sixteen target areas for long-range bombers in central and northeast Africa as well as the Persian Gulf region. These include Dakar, Freetown, Lagos, Aden, Port Sudan, Suez, Cairo, Alexandria, and Port Said.

Section VII, "Reconnaissance and military targets on the West Atlantic coast and in the USA," is the section of this plan with which we are most concerned. The text of this section reads as follows:

An examination of the armaments industry and the necessary raw material sources in the Western hemisphere will result in limited success at the 21 industrial targets listed (see pages 34/35). With this selection it should be considered: how many of these targets will fail (because of bombing raids), how many will experience backlogs in production (due to bombing raids), how many of these targets share production and what is the current supply available. In the last section of the list the percentages of total production are given for the end of 1942 and the beginning of 1943.

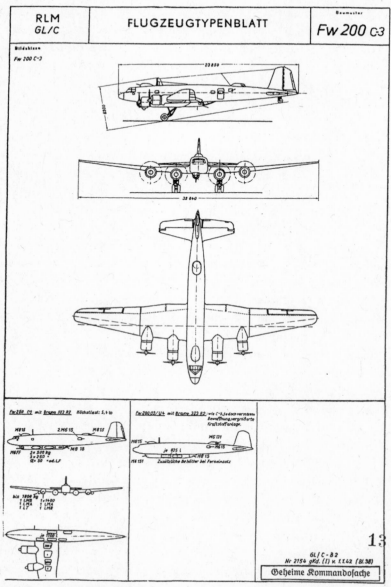

GL/C - B 2
Nr 2154 gKd. (I) v. 1.1.42 (81.38)
Geheime Kommandosache

German drawing of Fw 200.

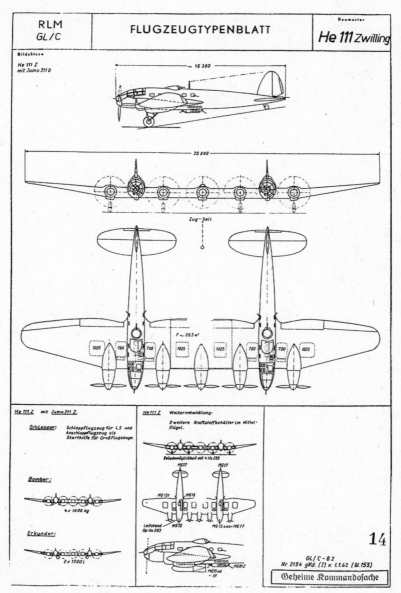

German drawing of He 111.

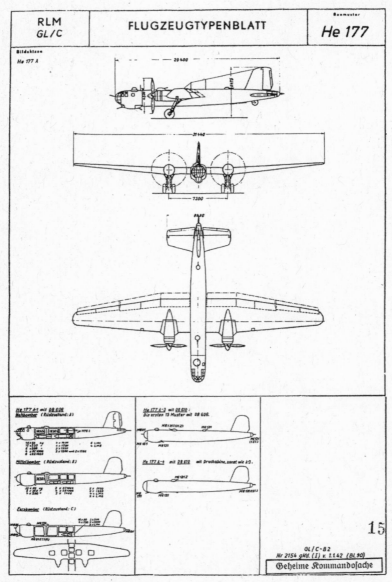

German drawing of He 177.

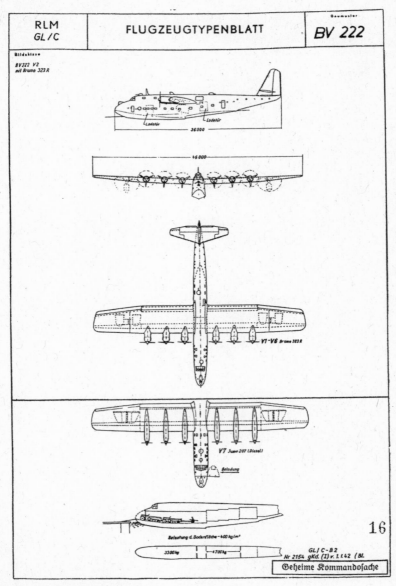

German drawing of BV 222.

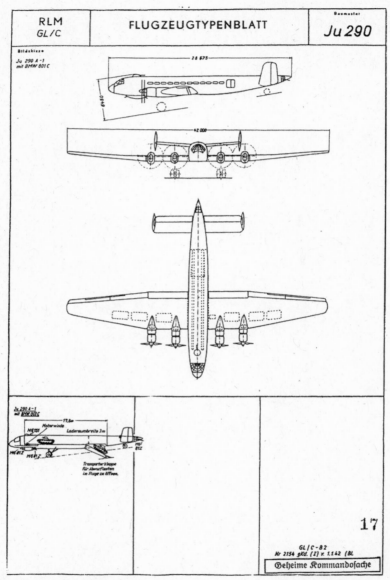

Bildskizze

Ju 290 A-1
mit BMW 801C

28 675

6950

42 000

Ju 290 A-1
mit BMW 801C

17,8m

Motorwinde

MG151

Laderaumbreite 3m

MG
151

MG 151

MG 151

Transporterklappe
Für Abwurflasten
im Fluge zu öffnen.

17

German drawing of Ju 290.

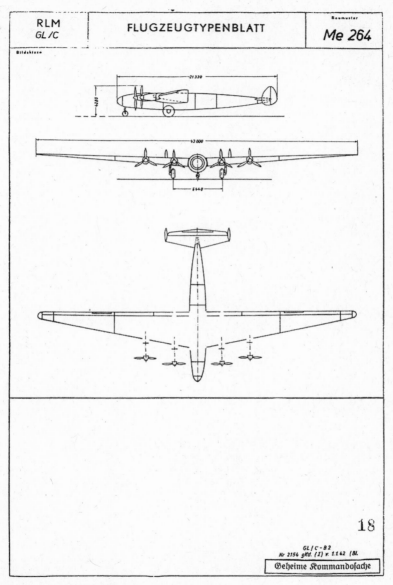

German drawing of Me 264.

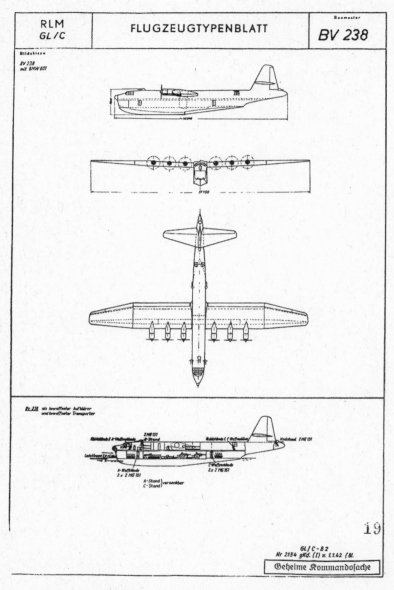

German drawing of BV 238.

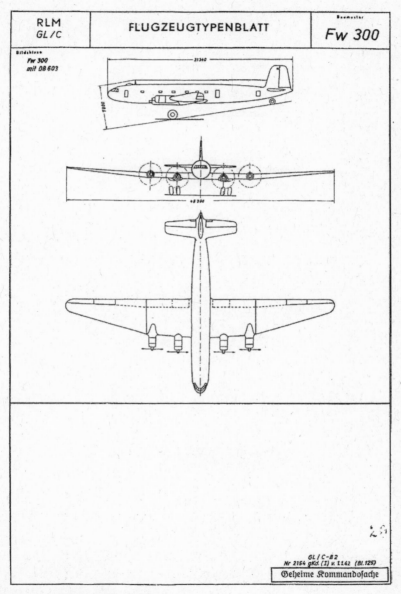

German drawing of Fw 300.

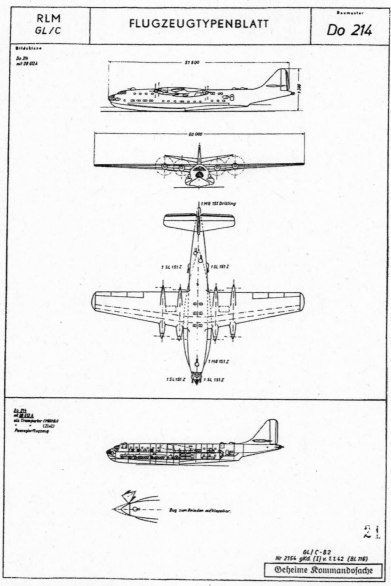

German drawing of Do 214.

## TABLE 1
## POTENTIAL TARGETS IN THE UNITED STATES

| Company | Product | City | State | Target # |
|---|---|---|---|---|
| Aluminum Corp of America | Aluminum | Alcoa | TN | 201 |
| Aluminum Corp of America | Aluminum | Massena | NY | 202 |
| Aluminum Corp of America | Aluminum | Badin | NC | 204 |
| Wright Aeronautical Corp | Aircraft Engines | Paterson | NJ | 205 |
| Pratt & Whitney Aircraft | Aircraft Engines | E. Hartford | CT | 206 |
| Allison Div of G.M. | Aircraft Engines | Indianapolis | IN | 207 |
| Wright Aeronautical Corp | Aircraft Engines | Cincinnati | OH | 208 |
| Hamilton Standard Corp | Aircraft Propellers | E. Hartford | CT | 209 |
| Hamilton Standard Corp | Aircraft Propellers | Pawcatuck | CT | 210 |
| Curtiss Wright Corp | Aircraft Propellers | Beaver | PA | 211 |
| Curtiss Wright Corp | Aircraft Propellers | Caldwell | NJ | 212 |
| Sperry Gyroscope Co. | Instruments | Brooklyn | NY | 213 |
| Cryolite Refinery | Cryolite Processing | Pittsburgh | PA | 215 |
| American Car & Foundry | Tanks | Berwick | PA | 216 |
| Colt Manufacturing | Artillery & Guns | Hartford | CT | 217 |
| Chrysler Corp | Tanks | Detroit | MI | 218 |
| Allis Chalmers | Anti-Aircraft Guns | La Porte | IN | 219 |
| Corning Glass Works | Various Lenses | Corning | NY | 220 |
| Bausch & Lomb | Various Lenses | Rochester | NY | 221 |

It should especially be mentioned that the refining and output of natural cryolite comes exclusively from Greenland and is used in the production of aluminum.

Regarding the condition of power plants, it is concluded that:

1. In the USA the completion of power plants since 1933 has been strongly promoted by the government.
2. Each power plant is connected to another by an extensive relay system.
3. The loss of 4 or 5 of the larger power plants [to a bombing campaign] will have little or no effect on armaments production since the energy use for civilian goods production exceeds the potential for meaningful cutbacks if necessary.[16]

Included in this section is a chart bearing the title: "Important Armament Facilities on the West Atlantic Coast and in The USA." The chart contains twenty-one targets, of which nineteen are located in the United States. One target is located near the southern tip of Greenland. The importance of this target is based on the fact that cryolite, a mineral vital to the production of aluminum, was at the time found primarily in Greenland. The other non-U.S. target is an aluminum plant in Vancouver, Canada. Aluminum was required for the manufacturing of aircraft.

Table 1, listing the American targets, contains the names of the companies being targeted, the products they manufactured that were required for the Allied war effort, and the city and state in which the facilities were located. The number following each target corresponds to numbers on the map that was part of the plan.

We can infer from the list that the goal was to cripple the American ability to manufacture large numbers of aircraft. Factories processing aluminum for airplane bodies, those producing engines and propellers to drive bombers and fighters, and glassworks making lenses for instruments including bombsights were the primary targets.

Section VIII, "1 world map showing the targets, the routes, and the distances," is the final section of the plan. It is a brief description of the information on the map of the world attached to the plan. The map contains the numbers corresponding to the listings in various sections of the proposed targets, including those in the United States. It also shows the air routes to be taken to those targets, as well as the aircraft type the planners recommended for each mission. Included is data on refueling aircraft either in flight or at sea.

Looking back with hindsight at the goals enumerated in this plan, we can see the flaws in the plan and the extreme optimism of the men who prepared it. But, taking into consideration the perspective of men whose nation had conquered most of Europe in a short period of time, and seemed virtually invincible and capable of developing whatever technology was required for military success, it is easier to understand how they could plan to attack a nation halfway across the world, and expect to succeed.

# CHAPTER 4

# The Race to Build the America Bomber

FROM THE END OF THE WAR OF 1812 UNTIL THE POST–WORLD WAR II era, the continental United States remained substantially immune from direct military attack by European and Asian powers. The age of intercontinental ballistic missiles, long-range bombers, and missiles fired from submarines changed that. Suddenly missiles fired from deep within the Soviet Union could reach American population centers, fleets of swift bombers could quickly darken the skies over our cities, and Soviet nuclear-powered submarines were patrolling off our coasts. An enemy now had the potential of bringing the terror and horrors of modern warfare to our very homes.

One of the earliest references we have of the Nazi desire to launch fleets of bombers against the United States is contained in a speech given by Hermann Göring, head of the Luftwaffe, on July 8, 1938. Göring told a gathering of representatives of the German aircraft manufacturing industry, "I completely lack the bombers capable of round-trip flights to New York with a 5-ton bomb load. I would be extremely happy to possess such a bomber which would at last stuff the mouth of arrogance across the sea." This meeting took place more than three years before the attack on Pearl Harbor brought America into the war.[1]

## "CHUCK A FEW BOMBS AT THEM"
The daring daylight bombing raids on German cities by aircraft of the U.S. Army Air Forces that began in May 1943 proved especially galling to the highest-ranking German officials. By using bases in Great Britain,

the Americans could attack Germany's cities without fear of retaliation by the Luftwaffe. This immunity to air attack granted by the vast expanse of the Atlantic Ocean never ceased to disturb Adolf Hitler, and especially Reich Marshal Göring. In his history of the German Air Force, David Irving wrote that Göring "would dearly have loved to bomb America."[2]

Göring's frustration over his inability to respond in kind to bombings from American aircraft was recorded in a meeting he had with the famous aircraft designer Willy Messerschmitt on October 14, 1943. Professor Messerschmitt was telling Göring about a new long-range bomber that he claimed was going to be capable of delivering as much as several tons of bombs to targets in the United States from European bases. Göring responded with a sigh, "If only we could do that! If only we could chuck a few bombs at them, so that they had to have a blackout over there...."[3]

Perhaps the Reich Marshal was recalling the Doolittle raid on Japan in April 1942. Just five months after the devastating attack on Pearl Harbor, sixteen B-25 medium bombers took off from a U.S. Navy aircraft carrier and bombed several cities on the Japanese home islands. The targets included the capital of Tokyo. Although the raid had no significant military value, it did serve to boost American morale and warned the enemy that the war could be brought to their homes. The Japanese public was reported to be stunned and shaken by the relative ease with which Colonel Doolittle and his pilots penetrated Japan's supposedly impenetrable defenses. At a time when the skies over Germany were filled with flights of hundreds of enemy bombers, perhaps Göring was hoping a small bombing raid on New York City would have the same effect on the American public that the Doolittle raid had on the Japanese.

Göring wasn't the only official thinking along those lines. U.S. Secretary of War Henry L. Stimson considered a reprisal raid on American cities by Japanese bombers "inevitable." *The New York Times* reported that "extraordinary precautions are being made to build up defenses" against just such a surprise attack. As for Secretary Stimson, he believed that the Japanese could target even cities along the East Coast. On May 28, 1942, he told a press conference, "An attack on Washington" in retaliation for the attack on Tokyo "is not wholly inconceivable."[4]

Looking back from the vantage point of sixty years, we can safely say that Nazi Germany had little chance of launching a full-scale invasion, or even a successful air raid, against the United States—maybe. Things looked a lot different in the years preceding and following the attack on Pearl Harbor, especially when Americans considered how unprepared our nation was for war.

Even after the war in Europe had begun, resistance to American participation was so strong that on April 3, 1940, the House Appropriations Committee slashed the armed forces' budget by nearly 10 percent. This resulted in the cancellation of two-thirds of the planned construction of 166 aircraft.[5]

In early May 1940, when the German Army began smashing its way west through Holland, Belgium, and France, the American Army was incapable of fielding more than a third of the divisions that tiny Belgium was using for her failing defense. The U.S. Army Air Corps had available for its use fifty heavy bombers and 150 fighters. The floodgate of funds to build an army and a navy capable of at least defending the United States did not open until a German victory in the west appeared obvious.[6]

In August 1940, German bombers rained death and destruction on London. Journalist Edward R. Morrow brought the daily events of the British capital at war into American homes through his radio broadcast, *London After Dark.* On the twenty-fourth of that month, the popular American magazine *Liberty* began publication of a series of thirteen installments of a novel that shocked its readers. Titled *Lightning in the Night,* the novel was written by Fred Allhoff, allegedly with the assistance of a general and an admiral. In the second chapter the United States is brought into the war by a combined Japanese and Soviet attack on Pearl Harbor. This is followed by an invasion of the West Coast and the German occupation of the Panama Canal. By the seventh chapter, bombs are falling on New York City just as they were that same day on London. The series had such an impact on the American public that the Berlin propaganda machine saw fit to attack it as an "outlandish exaggeration." By the time of the last installment, November 16, 1940, a full year before the Japanese attack on Pearl Harbor, *Liberty*'s newsstand sales had reached an all-time high. The novel was published in book form years later.[7]

Following the actual attack on Pearl Harbor on December 7, 1941, newspapers around the country reported sightings of Japanese submarines and other warships off the American West Coast. For the most part these were the result of fear and vivid imaginations. But, the very real concern about a second Japanese air attack, this one against aircraft manufacturing facilities in California, prompted the federal government to take unusual defensive measures. These included placing antiaircraft guns in the Hollywood hills, and installing barbed-wire barriers along beaches in Puget Sound. No one expected that such actions could sufficiently defend against an attack of the magnitude of the one that was launched against Hawaii, or could prevent a landing by Japanese troops.

After years of shrinking the size of our armed forces, and reducing weapons research and development budgets, the United States was unprepared for fighting a war of virtually any kind, much less one on two fronts. The condition of the American fighting forces at the time was aptly and frighteningly described by one of the Marine Corps' greatest wartime leaders, Lt. General Holland M. "Howling Mad" Smith: ". . . if the Japanese had continued from Pearl Harbor with an amphibious force and landed on the West Coast they would have found that we did not have enough ammunition to fight a day's battle. This is how close the country was to disaster in 1941."[8]

Fear that the Japanese would indeed continue to the West Coast caused a great deal of apprehension and resulted in widespread rumors of attacks by Japanese bombers, including a widely reported attack on Los Angeles on February 24–25, 1942. Reports of unidentified aircraft sightings caused nervous antiaircraft batteries to occasionally fill the California skies with explosions, which in turn increased the reports of attacks.[9]

The Japanese weren't the only ones stirring up fear of an air attack against the mainland of the United States. Even though Germany would not declare war against the United States for two more days, "On 9 December a report of a German air raid reached Naval Operating Base (NOB), Newport, Rhode Island, where the cruiser USS *Augusta* went to general quarters."[10]

The destruction of a major portion of the Pacific Fleet at Pearl Harbor awakened Americans to how vulnerable they were to enemy aircraft. "Rumors soon circulated that German submarines carrying light attack planes lurked off the east coast and that Germany might seize the French aircraft carrier the *Bearn* anchored in the West Indies," and use it to launch attacks on eastern cities.[11]

Concern that the Vichy French forces on Martinique might turn the Bearn and several other warships over to the Germans for use in an attack on the United States resulted in an order from President Roosevelt that the French remove enough specific machinery from the ships to make them immobile "within 36 hours" or be subjected to an American bombing raid. The job was accomplished in the allotted time.[12]

As we know, German bombing attacks along the East Coast never materialized. There are many reasons for this. One is that Germany never possessed a fleet of long-range heavy bombers capable of making the flight from Europe to the United States and back. This was not from a lack of desire. The obsession with finding an airplane that could reach and bomb the United States cost the German Third Reich an enormous amount of money, and consumed tremendous resources and manpower. The aircraft Willy Messerschmitt was telling Göring about when the latter made his comment about wanting to "chuck a few bombs at them," was the Me 264. Messerschmitt called it his "America Bomber." As we will see later in this chapter, it was not the only plane to acquire that nickname. In mid-October 1943 the designer was reviewing the Me 264 project with Göring when he assured him that when completed, the long-range aircraft would be capable of carrying several tons of bombs into the American heartland and returning. Actually, the project had been ongoing for a long time. It began when Hitler himself was shown a mock-up of the Me 264 in 1937.[13]

The absence of a long-range heavy bomber like Messerschmitt's "America Bomber" was one of the Luftwaffe's major shortcomings in the war. Field Marshal Erhard Milch, who held the post of Air Inspector General in the Luftwaffe from 1941 through 1944, made this fact clear. After the war, Milch wrote, "Germany had no really adequate aircraft model for use in strategic operations."[14]

## General Wever and the Uralbomber

The primary reason an otherwise modern air force lacked this vital component is that the one man who had both the vision and the power to build such a fleet died before the war began. Lt. General Walther Wever is usually not found in books about the Second World War, yet his strategic vision might have altered the outcome of the war, had he lived long enough.

Wever was the product of a middle-class family from the eastern province of Posen. He became an infantry officer candidate when he turned eighteen. After completing his training, he was commissioned a second lieutenant, a rank he held through the beginning of the First World War. Wever's service as a front-line platoon commander led to his promotion to captain, and eventually to a post on the staff of General Erich Ludendorf. While on the staff, he is credited with helping develop the "elastic defense" strategy used by the German Army to great advantage during the war. This allowed "forward areas to be temporarily abandoned during bombardments, leaving the strategic mass deep in dugouts and secure—that was responsible for breaking the back of the French army in the abortive Chemin des Dames offensive."[15]

During the interwar years he was in charge of training and rose to the rank of colonel. In 1932 Wever was appointed to the post of chief of the Air Command Office, a title that hid his real responsibility from the watchful eyes of Allied agents enforcing treaty rules against the establishment of a German air force. He was in reality the Chief of the Air General Staff.[16]

An infantry officer with no flying experience might at first appear an odd choice for chief of staff of an air force, but this drawback was more than compensated for by the forty-six-year-old Wever's reputation as a man "whose character and sense of mission were beyond question," and a man who could create and lead "a skilled and smoothly functioning staff." Army General Werner von Blomberg complained about the transfer of Wever to the air force by exclaiming, "You're taking my best man."[17]

Even before the war began, Wever anticipated Germany's future need for long-range heavy bombers. In 1934 he had specifications drawn for just such an aircraft. Wever wanted a four-engine bomber that could carry a bomb load of at least 3,300 pounds a distance of at least 1,243 miles, deliver its payload, and return. Because he expected the targets of such a bomber to be the Soviet production centers near the eastern end of European Russia and along the Ural Mountains, it became known as the "Uralbomber."[18]

In Wever's vision, the air force was to be more than an air arm in support of ground forces. He saw his objective as being the destruction of the enemy's means of war production, "the armament industry." Instead of trying to destroy an enemy's air force in air battles, he wanted to annihilate the factories in which aircraft and engines were manufactured. In a speech to the first graduating class of the Air War College that he had established, he explained that an air force operated with a weapon that had no boundaries. The targets of an air force, he said, "are not restricted to the fronts of the Army; they are above and behind the Army, over the coasts and seas, over the whole nation, and over the enemy's territories." The natural boundaries that slowed down the advance of an army, such as mountains and rivers, were no impediment to an air force. He capped his speech with a warning that would echo throughout the war years, "only the nation with strong bomber forces at its disposal can expect decisive action by its air force."[19]

The Luftwaffe Chief of Staff wasn't the first to describe the strategic missions of an air service. In December 1918, the British Chief of the Air Staff, Sir Frederick Sykes, said much the same thing: "Future wars between civilized nations will be struggles for life in which entire populations, together with their industrial resources, will be thrown into the scale. . . . The objectives of striking forces will be nerve centers, the armies and navies of the opponent, the population as a whole, his national morale and the industries without which he cannot wage war."[20]

It is important to keep in mind that Wever was not simply an advocate of a strong strategic long-range bomber force, but a powerful backer of a mixed-mission Luftwaffe, one comprised of heavy, medium, and light bombers, as well as dive-bombers and an entire array of fighters and other aircraft that could operate in support of ground forces. He saw the Luftwaffe as both a tactical and a strategic air force.

Wever's views were definitely in a minority among Germany's military leaders. Most viewed the primary job of an air force as operating in support of an advancing army. The majority viewpoint saw little use for a level, especially high-level, bomber. They learned differently when the skies above German cities were darkened by thousands of high-level bombers raining death and destruction on the Reich and her population.

In May 1936, Wever had the first Luftwaffe training manual published. It declared that "[a]ir power carries the war right into the heart of enemy country. . . . It strikes at the very root of the enemy's fighting power and of the people's will to resist." On the other hand, the manual clearly stated that bombing raids on cities "for the purpose of terrorizing the civilian population are absolutely forbidden."[21]

Contracts for the construction of four-engine, long-range heavy bombers were awarded to two German companies in late 1934, Dornier and Junkers. Based on plans drawn up under the watchful eye of Wever and his closest staff, which included the head of the Technical Department, Colonel Wilhelm Wimmer, work began immediately. On January 3, 1935, Dr. Heinrich Koppenberg, chairman of Junkers, reported that preliminary work on the Junkers version, the Ju 89, had been completed.[22]

The Dornier version, designated the Do 19, made its first successful flight on October 28, 1936. Two months later the Ju 89 made its maiden flight, but by then fate had reduced the priority of a four-engine long-range heavy bomber considerably.

On June 3, 1936, Wever was in Dresden for a speech to Luftwaffe cadets. He rushed to the nearby airfield for a flight back to Berlin to attend the funeral of a First World War hero. He was in the habit of piloting his own aircraft, and on this day he was using an airplane he was not entirely familiar with, a He 70 Blitz. As the plane lifted off, the ground crew watched in horror as one wing dipped dangerously close to the ground. Suddenly the aircraft appeared to be out of control as it turned downward itself and crashed in a fiery ball. Wever and his flight engineer were both killed.[23]

The vision of building a fleet of strategic long-range heavy bombers died along with Wever, at least for the time being. Wever's passing resulted in Germany's falling behind her future adversaries in the development of this vital type of bomber. During this same period the Boeing B-17, a long-range heavy bomber, was being developed in the United States, the same plane that would fill the skies over German cities during the last two years of the war.[24]

Following Wever's death, the leadership rudder came off the Luftwaffe as a series of former army officers ran the service with the constant interference of the inept Göring. General Albert Kesselring succeeded Wever as chief of staff. Perhaps because he was a former artilleryman, Kesselring was an advocate of the dominant view within the German armed services that the Luftwaffe's primary function was in support of ground forces. Therefore, a long-range heavy bomber and the concept of strategic bombing missions were not appropriate to the air service's mission. The "Uralbomber" project was ended on April 29, 1937. Göring is said to have decided against continued work on a long-range heavy bomber in favor of advancing work on developing medium bombers because he could build two and a half of the latter with the same resources required to build the former. Göring was like many of the Nazi leaders, enamored of the numbers. One hundred heavy long-range bombers would just not look as good on paper as two hundred and fifty medium bombers would, regardless of their performance or mission.[25]

On this very point, long-range heavy bombers versus shorter-range medium bombers, Göring is quoted as saying: "The Fuhrer does not ask me how big my bombers are, but how many they are."[26]

Three airplanes had been built and flown for the "Uralbomber" project. The Dornier remained in service as a transport until 1938. The two Junkers were also converted to use as transports, but both were lost during the invasion of Norway. A third partially completed Junkers was used as the basis for a new passenger plane, the Ju 90.[27]

From this point on the Luftwaffe was under the control of men who were committed to the role of the dive-bomber, to the detriment of long-range level bombers. Even the two-engine Ju 88, arguably the most versatile German aircraft of the war, was delayed in development because of the insistence that it be capable of operating as a dive-bomber in addition to being a level bomber.

Kesselring, who would later distinguish himself as an army commander, lasted little more than a year as Luftwaffe chief of staff. General Hans-Jurgen Stumpff, a former infantry officer, who remained in the post only slightly longer than Kesselring, replaced him. On February 1, 1939, one-time cavalry officer General Hans Jeschonnek was given the post. Jeschonnek had transferred to the air service as a staff officer in 1933. He remained as chief of staff until August 1943. Under increasing pressure from Hitler, who blamed him rather than his friend Göring for the failure of the Luftwaffe to live up to expectations, he shot himself in the head while seated at his desk. He left a note requesting that Göring not attend his funeral. Göring ignored the request.[28]

Military historians Benjamin King and Timothy Kutta describe Jeschonnek as "[a] man totally dedicated to his profession and personally above reproach," but also "the wrong man for the job."[29]

Jeschonnek was the wrong man for several reasons, one of which was his belief in the infallibility of Adolf Hitler. But even worse was his adherence to the obsessive belief in dive-bombers held by one of his subordinates, Lieutenant General Ernst Udet. A fighter ace in the First World War, Udet was director of the Luftwaffe's Technical Department. Shortly after Wever's death, Göring had removed Wimmer, an advocate of Wever's strategic bomber program, from that post and personally selected Udet. His passion for dive-bombers began while on a visit to the United States in 1933. On September 27 he was in Buffalo, New York, touring the Curtiss-Wright aircraft factory when Glenn L. Curtiss asked the former ace if he would like to pilot one of the planes then rolling off the assembly line. The aircraft was the F2C Hawk biplane, built for the U.S. Navy as a carrier-based dive-bomber. Udet realized that this aircraft was the navy's answer to bombing that most elusive of all targets, a moving ship. After the flight, which included a 250-mile-per-hour plunge toward an imaginary target, the exuberant Udet immediately contacted Berlin for permission to purchase two of them. The two Hawks were soon on their way to Germany, and they became the basis on which future German dive-bombers were based.[30]

That visit by Udet began his obsession, which would ultimately become the fatal flaw of the Luftwaffe. Using his influence as the director of the Technical Department, he demanded that all bombers be able to perform their role while in a deep dive. Even the much heralded and anxiously awaited four-engine He 177 long-range heavy bomber was delayed in production when it was badly needed because Udet had told the manufacturer, Dr. Ernst Heinkel, that the plane had no future unless it could operate as a dive-bomber.[31]

Although not intended as a transatlantic aircraft, the He 177 had caught everyone's imagination as the long-range heavy bomber Germany sorely lacked. Unfortunately for the Luftwaffe, it never fulfilled its promise, earning instead the nickname "flaming coffin" among pilots. Its unusual engine configuration, two engines coupled together on each wing so it appeared to be a two-engine craft, never really worked well. They were prone to overheating and bursting into flames.[32]

## THE RACE FOR THE BOMBER
Despite the direction the Luftwaffe took following the loss of Wever, Hitler, the ultimate decision maker in the Third Reich, was still captivated with the idea of big, heavy, long-range bombers that could strike at distant targets and return safely to their bases. The first work on an "America Bomber" capable of reaching the United States was begun by the aircraft designer whom Hitler considered "a genius," Professor Willy Messerschmitt. Field Marshal Erhard Milch's biographer reports that Milch did not share the Fuhrer's opinion of Messerschmitt, and was opposed to his company participating in the race to build a bomber intended for attacks on the United States. Milch believed that job should be left to Junkers and Dornier.[33]

As in many other areas in Nazi Germany, politics and personalities took their toll on aircraft technological advancements. Milch and Messerschmitt were constantly at odds with each other during most of the war years, each blaming the other for various failures. Their personal animosity dated from 1928, when Milch was a director of Lufthansa and Messerschmitt had failed to meet an important contract. Professor Hugo Junkers had also proved to be an intractable foe of Milch's ideas, but he had solved that problem by forcing the old man out and taking control of his company for the Luftwaffe. Milch clearly favored the aircraft manufacturer he could control rather than the one headed by a man who appeared to oppose him at every step. Even after the war, while they were prisoners of the Allies, they continued their feud.

Specifications were first prepared in 1937, and enlarged on the following year, for an aircraft of incredible, for that time, performance. The goal was to build a multifunctional aircraft that could deliver a five-ton bomb load to New York City and a smaller bomb load to targets in the central part of the United States, and make reconnaissance patrols as far as the American West Coast. Gerhard Weinberg reports that within the German government circles that were knowledgeable of these plans, the aircraft was referred to as both the "America Bomber," and the "New York Bomber."[34]

It is probable that the memory of Messerschmitt showing him, in 1939, the mock-up of his Me 264 long-range bombers that could reach the United States was never far from Hitler's consciousness. The Fuhrer loved miraculous weapons, and from his perspective an airplane that could carry a bomb load that far was indeed a miracle. From that time on, "Hitler had been calling for an airplane capable of bombing the United States. . . ."[35]

Hitler's goal was to have a plane that could fly out of central Europe, bomb targets in the United States, and return to Europe without the need for refueling. Later in the war the American air forces considered the same mission in reverse, but approached it differently. Whereas the Germans attempted to accomplish this goal in one step—the building of a bomber with extraordinary range—the Americans used a two-step approach, which resulted in first the B-29 and then the B-36.

Messerschmitt received a contract to build its "America Bomber" in 1940. The Fuhrer was so "optimistic about the prospects of the bomber" that in June 1941 he told Mussolini that it would be in full production by the end of that year.[36]

At least three other aircraft companies joined Messerschmitt in the quest to build Hitler's "America Bomber." These included Junkers, Heinkel, and Focke-Wulf. All four of these companies had produced warplanes that operated successfully during the war. Several of the planes that were proposed never quite lived up to the range requirements for a transoceanic bombing mission, but each of these manufacturers made their best attempt to meet the Fuhrer's goal. Let's review the progress made by each of these companies in building the "America Bomber."

## MESSERSCHMITT—ME 264

The Me 264 was the first aircraft to acquire the name "America Bomber." Willy Messerschmitt was so enthused by Hitler's reaction to the mock-up the aircraft designer showed him that he worked on its development for three years before receiving an actual government contract.

The original concept work for the Me 264 was known as Project 1061. The goal was to build a four-engine aircraft capable of operating at a range of 12,428 miles. The project was begun in 1937, but due to the increased demands for more traditional aircraft, especially the single-engine fighter Bf 109, and the twin-engine night fighter Bf 110, work was done only intermittently. The company was originally named Bayerische Flugzeugwerke, but was changed to Messerschmitt when Willy Messerschmitt was appointed chairman and managing director in July 1938.

The priority of Project 1061 changed on August 10, 1940, when the German Navy wrote to Göring, telling him that the planned occupation of colonies in central Africa would require a bomber/transport with a range of 3,728 miles. About the same time, the Air Ministry issued its requirements for a long-range aircraft that would be capable of flying from bases in France to the United States for anticipated bombing raids. The expected range of such a round-trip was set at 7,457 miles. A few days before Christmas Messerschmitt told the three designers working on Project 1061, Wolfgang Degel, Paul Konrad, and Waldemar Voigt, that the plane would need the range requirement they had originally planned on, 12,428 miles. It would also have to be able to deliver in excess of eleven thousand pounds of bombs in an internal bomb bay, as well as an assortment of small bombs hung under its wings.

Soon thereafter, Messerschmitt received the order to build six prototypes of this most extraordinary aircraft. Project 1061 was changed and the craft was given the designation Me 264. The company was informed that if the Me 264 met all the performance ratings that Messerschmitt claimed, an additional twenty-four planes for "harassing missions against the United States" would be ordered.

In the meantime, Messerschmitt was also working on a six-engine version of the same aircraft that he hoped would exceed the range and payload expectations of the four-engine aircraft under construction.

On January 22, 1941, the Luftwaffe General Staff called for testing on a variety of proposed aircraft that could operate at long distances over the Atlantic Ocean in support of the U-boat campaign against shipping between the United States and Great Britain. In addition to the Me 264, three other airplanes were to be compared for this task, the He 177, the six-engine float plane BV 222, and the Focke-Wulf Fw 200. A prototype of the latter had made a record-setting nonstop flight from Berlin to New York in slightly less than twenty-five hours in August 1938 on behalf of Lufthansa. It then made the return trip a few days later in nineteen hours and fifty-five minutes. This was a stripped-down version with no armament and no payload.[37]

The Me 264 remained the favored aircraft for a trans-Atlantic bombing campaign. To help improve its performance, the Luftwaffe's Technical Department worked on various plans they had developed for the plane. These included an in-flight refueling system, and using six engines instead of four. There were also suggestions for using one group of Me 264s to tow a second group out to midocean and release them for their own self-propelled flight to the United States.

Debate continued within the Luftwaffe concerning the actual performance that could be expected of the Me 264. Some questioned the range possible with only four engines, which prompted Messerschmitt to begin talking about his plane less for taking on bombing raids against U.S. cities and more as a weapon for long-range "Atlantic missions," such as locating convoys for the U-boat fleets and arming the plane with missiles for use against Allied naval vessels.

In April 1942, a commission headed by Lt. Colonel Peterson visited the Messerschmitt plant in Augsburg and reviewed all the detailed plans and specs of the aircraft. His report estimated that the Me 264 could be ready for attacks against the United States by the fall of 1943. Meanwhile

The Messerschmitt America Bomber, Me 264. *USED WITH PERMISSION OF MARK SAN-SOM, GERMAN MILITARIA & COLLECTIBLES, WWW.GERMAN-MILITARIA.CO.UK.*

Me 264 America Bomber in flight over New York City. *USED WITH PERMISSION AND THANKS TO FILIP ZOUBEK OF MPM LTD.*

the original order for six test models was reduced to three as part of the rush to find the plane that could accomplish the mission and also to meet other aircraft requirements needed to combat the worsening war situation, now that the United States had joined the British bombing campaign against Germany.

Delays in the delivery of components continued, as did doubts about Messerschmitt's performance claims for his new plane. At one point during late spring 1942, Air Ministry officials decided that for any aircraft

Cockpit of the Me 264 America Bomber. *USED WITH PERMISSION AND THANKS TO CHARLES BAIN.*

Scale model of Me 264 America Bomber from original plans. *USED WITH PERMISSION AND THANKS TO MATTHIAS SIMON, AIRMODEL PRODUCTS.*

to be able to fly from France to the American East Coast for a bombing raid and return to base—they were now calling this the "America-Case"—it would have to be refueled in midflight. This had already been tested successfully with an Fw 58 and a Ju 90. Despite the success of this refueling in flight, General Jeschonnek remained opposed to this option.

By now Milch was getting fed up with the High Command's lack of enthusiasm for new technologies such as midflight refueling, so he ordered all work being done on this most important part of long-distance flights halted.

The Me 264 received a badly needed boost on May 19 through General Freiherr von Gablenz, a lifelong friend and greatly trusted ally of Milch. Gablenz had conducted his own study of the aircraft. His recommendation was that because the plane was so technologically advanced, it was an important step in the future of aviation, and as such, work should continue on its development. In fact, he recommended that plans be instituted to build thirty of them, both heavily armed and armored for combat, and lightly armed for long-distance bombing missions.

At an August 7 meeting, Göring appeared to at least temporarily drop his demand for a rushed bombing raid on the United States by the Me 264, and instead pressed for its use as a midocean convoy spotter for U-boats.

Finally, on December 23, 1942, the first Me 264, dubbed V1, was test flown. Test flights continued as improvements were made on such things as the landing gears. It was now decided that the "America Bomber" Willy Messerschmitt had bragged about to Hitler back in 1939 might actually come into being by mid-1944. One serious problem, among many related to engine availability and component supplies, was that no aircraft facility could be located to actually manufacture the thirty large airplanes the plans called for. Every aircraft plant was already operating at or even above capacity turning out aircraft that were needed now for the defense of the Reich.

While the test flights of the one model of the Me 264 that had been completed continued, the dispute over the airplane's future continued. The navy did not want it for long-range sea reconnaissance. It preferred the Ta 400, which was still on the drawing board. In the meantime it urged that further construction of the Messerschmitt bombers be halted and work on the Ju 290 and the He 177 be advanced. Simultaneously, the Luftwaffe's Ordnance Department told Messerschmitt to hurry the completion of the two remaining Me 264s that had been contracted. Confusion reigned; if the plane's new primary objective was now to be used for so-called "Atlantic missions," searching out enemy convoys on the vast Atlantic, should work continue if the navy did not want it?

In June 1943, still with only one model completed and flying, Messerschmitt continued to pump Hitler with his stories of how much this bomber could accomplish for Germany. The following month the Fuhrer told Admiral Donitz, who was now commander in chief of the German Navy, that the Me 264s were "the machines" that would work in support of the submarines. It was at this time also that Hitler appeared finally to give up the idea of having these "America Bombers" attack the United States. His reason was that with the prospect of only a few of them available, they could not do any real damage, and the only thing they would accomplish was to provoke the American people into greater effort against Germany.

Work on improving the one existing model of the Messerschmitt "America Bomber" continued, as did efforts to improve the engines and armaments for the next two models, until July 1944. On the eighteenth of that month an Allied bombing raid destroyed the completed V-1, along with the partially completed V-2 and V-3 models. By September, Hitler was busy trying to find a way to keep the Allied armies from invading the Reich, and the idea of long-range reconnaissance flights in support of the diminishing U-boat fleets was of much less importance, so he agreed to cancel all work on the Me 264. On October 18, 1944, Reichsmarshal Technical Order No. 2 made the cancellation official.

Hitler's dream that his favored aircraft designer would build a fleet of bombers capable of attacking the United States homeland was crippled by infighting among Luftwaffe personalities, by lack of cooperation between the Luftwaffe and the navy, and most of all by Germany's inability to build the engines and the airframes that could accomplish the mission in the midst of a relentless Allied bombing campaign. This bombing reduced already short material supplies and ultimately destroyed the only working model that had been built.[38]

The Me 264 "America Bomber" had a wingspan of slightly over 141 feet, about the same as the American B-29, and approximately 30 feet longer than that of the B-24. Its fuselage was 66 feet long, about the same as the B-24's. Could it have accomplished the desired mission? Perhaps, had there been less stop-and-go involved in the design and construction work; had there been less infighting over the airplane, especially between General Field Marshal Milch and Willy Messerschmitt; and if the resources, particularly the reliable engines, had been available. Because so few test flights were made of the Me 264, the potential of this aircraft remains a point of dispute among aircraft designers and military historians to this day.

## JUNKERS—JU 390

While Willy Messerschmitt struggled to get his version of the "America Bomber" selected as the aircraft the Luftwaffe would use to meet Hitler's plans for land-based bomber raids on American cities, the Junkers Company worked on its variant.

Hugo Junkers had lost control of his company to the Nazi government in 1933 under the threat of imminent arrest. He died in 1935. The company was under the complete and direct control of the Luftwaffe, and as such was a favored manufacturer.

The Junkers Company had specialized in heavy-duty long-range airplanes. Its G-38, a four-engine passenger plane, at the time the largest commercial land-based plane in the world, made its first flight in late 1929. Two years later Lufthansa was using it, and a second model with a two-story fuselage, for regular passenger runs between Berlin and London and Berlin and Paris. The impressive-looking massive plane was a favorite of business travelers. The original G-38 was lost in a 1936 crash resulting from improper maintenance, but the second model went on to serve in the war as a transport plane until it was destroyed in May 1941 by British fighter-bombers while on the ground.[39]

As already noted, Junkers was one of the two companies in Germany with enough experience in building heavy aircraft to be awarded contracts to build prototypes of the "Uralbomber" for General Wever. The result of the Junkers effort was the Ju 89. Following Göring's cancellation of the Ju 89 as the proposed "Uralbomber," the partially completed third version of this aircraft went on to become the first Ju 90, a series of highly successful passenger planes used by Lufthansa. After the outbreak of the war the Ju 90 served as a heavy cargo plane in various theaters of operation. Improvements in design and engines led eventually to a new designation for this expanded aircraft. With the designation Ju 290, the various models of this plane that were built served a variety of needs. These included being used as a long-range maritime reconnaissance/bomber, and as a heavy transport and heavy bomber. With a cruising speed of 220 miles per hour, it could operate at a range of 3,784 miles. The Ju 290 had the capacity to carry a bomb load in excess of six thousand pounds, or three antiship missiles.[40]

Junkers responded to Hitler's call for an "America Bomber" with a plan to use the Ju 290 as the basis for an aircraft capable of carrying an acceptable bomb load to the United States and returning to Europe. Just as the Ju 89 "Uralbomber" became the Ju 90 transport, then the Ju 290 long-range reconnaissance/bomber, it finally reached its peak as the Ju 390 "America Bomber." In 1943 General Wever's dream of a large heavy-duty long-range bomber actually came into existence, but unfortunately for the Luftwaffe it was too late in the war to build more than two flying models.

Six 1,700-horsepower BMW engines powered the Ju 390. It had a wingspan of over 181 feet, and was 110 feet long. By comparison, the Ju 390 was eleven feet longer than the four-engine B-29, and her wings were forty feet wider. It was the largest land-based bomber built during the war on either side.

Junkers was awarded a contract to build two working models of the Ju 390. In many ways it was a promising development, since it made use of many components from the Ju 290 that had already been manufactured or at least had already been tested and approved. As a result, construction moved along rather quickly.

The first Ju 390, designated V-1, was test flown on October 20, 1943. The results proved satisfactory enough that the Air Ministry ordered that twenty-six more be built in addition to the two models originally ordered. The second prototype, V-2, made a successful test flight soon after. In

The Junkers America Bomber, Ju 390. *USED WITH PERMISSION OF MARK SANSOM, GERMAN MILITARIA & COLLECTIBLES, WWW.GERMAN-MILITARIA.CO.UK.*

Junkers America Bomber Ju 390 being prepared for flight. *USED WITH PERMISSION OF WWW.WARBIRDSRESOURCEGROUP.ORG.*

January 1944 it was assigned to the long-range maritime reconnaissance unit FAGr.5 at Mont de Marsan, south of Bordeaux. It was from here that the Ju 390 V-2 was said to have made a test run to the East Coast of the United States to substantiate the aircraft's ability for such a sustained nonstop flight. We examine more about this flight in Chapter 7.

No further Ju 390s were ever built. The two prototypes either were destroyed by Allied bombers, or were blown up by retreating German troops to keep them from falling into enemy hands. Following the Normandy invasion and the rapid loss of air bases close to the Atlantic, all long-range maritime reconnaissance units were withdrawn to Germany in mid-1944. The contracts for the twenty-six Ju 390s were cancelled in June of that year, and by September all work had ceased. By then the German aviation industry was focused on building fighters for defense of the homeland. Bombing New York was no longer an option for serious consideration for anyone with enough understanding of the war situation to realize that Germany was racing toward its own doom now that the Allies had landed in France and were moving east. What remained of the Luftwaffe was struggling to regain control of the airspace over Germany, and long-range bombers were now a luxury, while fighters were a necessity.

Reports concerning the potential performance of the Ju 390 vary significantly. An acceptable estimate of what a completed version used for long-range reconnaissance and possibly a bombing raid could accomplish puts it well within the realm of conducting a bombing raid from France against a city such as New York, given enough time to work out design problems and enough planes to conduct such an attack. The production models were to have a maximum speed of 314 miles per hour; a cruising speed of 222 miles per hour; and a range in the reconnaissance configuration of 6,000 miles. The bomber version, with a load of 4,255 pounds of bombs, had a range of 5,750 miles.[41]

## HEINKEL—HE 277

By the time the order to find a bomber capable of reaching the United States emanated from Hitler's headquarters, the company founded by Ernst Heinkel had already earned a reputation for success. This was based

Heinkel America Bomber He 277 sitting on a German runway. *PHOTO USED WITH PERMISSION OF LUFTWAFFEPICS.COM.*

on the He 111, a two-engine medium bomber that had become the backbone of the Luftwaffe's bomber arm. Boasting a top speed of 227 miles per hour and a range in excess of 1,200 miles, it was a common sight over England throughout the war.

Heinkel's reputation was severely damaged by the poor engine design used in the He 177, which coupled two engines together on each wing. The objective of this design was to reduce drag to help the large aircraft meet the unrealistic demand that it be able to operate as a dive-bomber. As already noted, this never worked well and often resulted in the engines overheating while in flight and catching fire. This earned the unfortunate aircraft the sobriquet "flaming coffin" among flight and ground crews.

When it came time to build a four-engine heavy bomber with transatlantic potential, the Heinkel designers dropped the engine coupling and moved to using the more traditional design of four independent engines. Despite the fact that Göring, who was fed up with the failures of the He 177, ordered Heinkel not to attempt to turn the plane into a true four-engine bomber, Heinkel's designers did exactly that, calling their project the He 177B. In early 1944 Heinkel told Hitler of his new four-engine long-range bomber and received the Fuhrer's support to build a series of them as quickly as possible.[42]

The plane's designation was quickly changed to He 277, and work was stepped up. The first prototype of this long-range heavy bomber made its first test flight in December 1943 as the He 177B. Refinements were worked out at a plant in Austria, and the hope was to have at least several serial models in production by the fall of 1944. But, all work on the He 277 came to an abrupt halt on July 3, 1944, when the order to focus on fighters went out to all aircraft manufacturers. It is believed that as many as eight of the He 277s were actually completed, but all were apparently lost to Allied bombings during the final year of the war. A few photographs of the He 277 survived the war, as well as some details concerning its performance and dimensions. There were two versions built, the V series and the B series, the second being the larger of the two. The B series He 277s were nearly 73 feet long, had a wingspan of slightly over 131 feet, were powered by four Jumo 213F engines (each with 2,060 horsepower), had a maximum speed of 354 miles per hour, and had an operational range of 4,474 miles.[43]

## FOCKE-WULF—TA 400

Founded in 1924 by Georg Wulf, Professor Heinrich Focke, and Dr. Werner Neumann in Bremen, Germany, the Focke-Wulf Aircraft Construction Company experienced moderate success with a series of light passenger airplanes used by several European airlines. The arrival of Kurt Tank in 1931 to assume leadership of the company's design department changed all that. Tank would become one of the world's leading aircraft designers and engineers.

During the war, Tank had designed and Focke-Wulf had built two of the most highly regarded aircraft in use by the Luftwaffe. The Fw 190 single-seat fighter was first introduced in 1941 as a replacement for the aging Me 109 fleets. It proved more than a match for the British Spitfires, then Britain's leading fighter. Many aircraft experts consider the Fw 190 one of the best single-seat fighters of the war.

A second Tank design was the Fw 200 Condor. A long-range reconnaissance bomber, the Condor became the Luftwaffe's chief antishipping weapon and scouting craft for the U-boats. Although less than three hundred of the four-engine Condors are thought to have been built, their

Artist's rendering of a flight of Focke-Wulf Ta 400 America Bombers. *USED WITH PERMISSION OF ARTIST SKIP TALBOT.*

cruising speed of 208 miles per hour, operational range in excess of 2,200 miles, and ability to remain aloft for fourteen hours, helped them become the scourge of Allied shipping. Its record of Allied shipping sunk by air attack is out of proportion with the number of Condors actually in service. It was an early version of the Condor that made the famous 1938 nonstop flight from Berlin to New York.

It was probably no surprise when Kurt Tank and Focke-Wulf decided to enter the competition to build the "America Bomber." Design work was begun on what the company called the Ta 400 in 1943. French technicians working in the Chatillon sur Begneux suburb southeast of Paris did much of the work. Contracts for the design and construction of major components were awarded to German, French, and Italian firms in an effort to speed up the process and begin building the first prototypes as quickly as possible.

The original design for the Ta 400 called for the use of six BMW radial engines, each producing 1,700 horsepower. This was later altered by the inclusion of two Jumo 004 jet engines. Because no prototype of the Ta 400 was ever built, it never got beyond construction of a wind tunnel model; the performance ranges and dimensions are based solely on the estimates of the designers. If one had been built, its wingspan would have been nearly 138 feet, and its overall length slightly over 95 feet. It was expected to achieve a maximum speed of 332 miles per hour, and have an operational range of close to 5,000 miles with a bomb load of approximately 22,000 pounds.[44]

## HORTEN BROTHERS—HO 18

Reimar and Walter Horten were not only brothers, but also aircraft designers who specialized in all-wing aircraft. Their prewar planes included gliders and sailplanes. Perhaps because both were also fighter pilots, most of their wartime design work was focused on all-wing fighter planes. Originally they were not included on the list of designers asked to submit ideas to the Air Ministry for an "America Bomber," but when they learned the large aircraft companies were experiencing difficulties achieving the desired range, they decided to try their hands at it. The result was the Ho 18, a 131-foot-wide flying wing powered by six Jumo 004B turbojet engines.

On February 25, 1945, they presented their design at a Berlin meeting. Soon thereafter Göring told them they would have to work with the engineers at Junkers to get their aircraft built. They quickly discovered that the Junkers designers had formed a committee with Messerschmitt designers and they planned on altering the original Horten designs.

Unhappy with the committee's recommended changes, Reimar made a series of his own that he felt would improve the craft's performance. His expectations were that this second version would achieve a maximum speed of 850 miles per hour, with a range of 6,835 miles. The flying wing "America Bomber" never got off the drawing board because the war ended soon after the planned beginning of the work on a prototype.[45]

For all the reasons already discussed, including personality differences and political jockeying, and the limitations of time and material resources, Germany never built the "America Bomber" Hitler had dreamed of during the early years of the war. The failure was definitely not from a lack of desire to both please the Fuhrer and strike at an enemy whose own bombers brought so much death and destruction to the Reich. It was just not meant to be.

# CHAPTER 5

# Rockets, Missiles, and the Nazi ICBM

IN THIS CHAPTER WE WILL EXAMINE THE DEVELOPMENT OF TWO NEW weapon systems invented by German scientists and technicians during the war, and how they were to be used against the United States. We will also reveal just how shockingly close these weapons actually came to being launched against American cities, and how those attacks could have occurred.

The first of these was the Flakzielgerat 76, known to those who designed and built it as the FZG 76. The first guided missile to be launched in large numbers, Hitler dubbed it the V-1. The V identified it as a vengeance weapon, used against Great Britain in reprisal for the Allied bombing of German cities. Because of the shrill, sputtering sound they made while in flight, the British population called these weapons "Buzz Bombs" and "Doodlebugs."

The second vengeance weapon was the V-2. This was a forty-six-foot-long rocket propelled by an engine fueled by a combination of liquid oxygen and alcohol. The V-2 was actually a series of rockets, each an improvement on its predecessor. The men who developed and launched the V-2 called the one most commonly fired at enemy targets the A4. The series ended with the A9 and the A10, both of which played a key role in targeting American cities.

For simplicity purposes, we will always refer to the FZG 76 as the V-1, but because of the difference in individual rocket performance and goals, and to avoid confusion, we will use both the V-2 name Hitler gave the army's rockets as well as each individual rocket's real designation, such as A4.

## The Birthplace of the Missile

The Peene River runs through the modern German state of Mecklenburg-Vorpommern in what once was the German Democratic Republic (East Germany). At the point where the river empties into the Baltic Sea, its right bank is composed of Usedom Island. In 1935 German scientists were searching for a location to build a combined army/Luftwaffe research center for the work each service was doing on the development of guided missiles and rockets. They needed a place where they could do the research, build the missiles and rockets, and test fire them. The latter would require a long-range area that did not include any populated areas. The obvious choice was along the Baltic coast, so the missiles and rockets could be fired down a range over the water.

Legend has it that Wernher von Braun, who was busily engaged in the search, was visiting his parents' farm in Silesia for Christmas that year and mentioned his search. His mother suggested he consider Usedom Island. The island consisted of mostly tree-covered dunes and was populated by more wildlife than people. It had the added feature of being more or less isolated from the local population. Wernher's grandfather used to duck hunt on the island.[1]

By 1935 Wernher von Braun had become something of a legendary figure, especially among those with an interest in rocketry and space travel. His interest in space travel began in 1920 when Wernher was eight years old. His mother, the Baroness Emmy von Quistrop, herself an accomplished astronomer, gave Wernher a telescope with which he could track the heavenly bodies. By the time he was thirteen he had set a goal that would consume the rest of his life, building a craft that could take a man to the moon and back. On the advice of Hermann Oberth, a Transylvanian schoolteacher whose book *The Rocket for Interplanetary Space* was published in 1923, Wernher pursued a course of studies centered on related sciences. He eventually earned degrees in physics and mathematics. When Wernher was about sixteen he joined an organization started by Oberth called the Society for Space Travel, which met regularly in the back room of a restaurant in Breslau.

As the Society grew in membership and expanded both its theoretical and practical research, it became clear it required a somewhat isolated and safe location to work and launch its rockets. Following several mishaps, one of which cost a member his life in an explosion, the Society leased an unused four-square-kilometer former army ammunition dump in a northern Berlin suburb in 1930. They called it the Raketenflugplatz (Rocket Flight Place), Berlin.

In the spring of 1932, three army officers dressed in civilian clothes visited the amateur rocketeers. Among them was Captain Walter Dornberger, an artillery officer with an MS in mechanical engineering. Dornberger was an outgoing, friendly smooth-talker. He has been described as a master salesman and an expert at bureaucratic maneuvering. He was also an extremely intelligent and farsighted engineer who was destined to move Germany's rocket and missile research from the planning table into reality and into the future.

Born in 1895 in the southwest German city of Giessen, Dornberger had a father who had been a pharmacist. His experience with heavy artillery units on the western front during the First World War led to his interest in ballistics. This eventually aroused an interest in the use of self-propelled rockets as substitutes for long-range artillery shells. In 1930 he joined the staff of the army Ordnance Testing Division. He specialized in rocket research, both liquid-fueled and solid-fueled rockets.[2]

At the time of his visit to the civilian rocketeers, Dornberger was in charge of the army's rocket development program, then working out of an artillery proving ground near Kummersdorf, south of Berlin. Impressed by the work and knowledge of the amateurs, Dornberger invited them to test fire one of their rockets at Kummersdorf, which they did with poor results in July.

Despite the failure of the test flight, Dornberger hired several of the amateurs, including von Braun, to work on the army's rocket program. He also arranged for von Braun to enroll at Friedrich-Wilhelm University, where he earned his PhD in physics.[3]

By 1935 Hitler was pouring enormous funds into building Germany's new army. Some of that money went into the rocket development program at Kummersdorf. With the testing of the first of the A series of rockets, the A2, it soon became apparent that the program had outgrown Kummersdorf. The extended range of this rocket meant it had to be transported to an island in the Baltic for firing since it became too dangerous for testing over populated areas. Soon the decision was made to move the entire operation to a location where all the research, building, and testing of the rockets could take place within the same facility. The solution was found in the tiny village of Peenemunde at the tip of Usedom Island.

At a June 27, 1935, meeting that included many experts in ballistics, munitions, and aircraft engines, von Braun presented a paper that historian Michael J. Neufeld calls "Peenemunde's birth certificate." In it he outlined a facility in which private companies would play a minor role, usually as subcontractors, instead of major participants as some had been urging. He wanted the research and development done by a combination of funding and manpower supplied by the Luftwaffe and the army. Each service could pursue its own work at the same shared facility: the army on its "free-flying liquid-fuel rocket," and the Luftwaffe on its "aircraft rocket engine." What he proposed was the creation of an "experimental rocket establishment," that could do its work in secret.[4]

Shaped somewhat like a human thumb, Usedom Island is approximately sixty-two miles long and twenty-eight miles wide. The Luftwaffe quickly purchased the site from the city of Wolgast, and clearing and construction began soon after. In an amazing example of interservice rivalry working to good advantage, funding flowed into the project from both the Luftwaffe and the army. When the army's Chief of Ordnance, General Karl Becker, learned that the Luftwaffe's Major Wolfram von Richthofen, a cousin of the famous Red Baron and head of the Technical Office's Development Division, had pledged five million reichsmarks to the construction project, he fumed and was determined that the air force would not become the senior partner in the rocket development program. He pledged an additional six million reichsmarks from the army.[5]

As things turned out, the Luftwaffe did not require a great deal of space at the new facility. The Luftwaffe's portion of the Peenemunde Experimental Center was located in the northwest corner of the island. It was called Peenemunde West. Within the approximately four square miles of Peenemunde West were an airfield intended for use by experimental aircraft, an administrative building, and the research facility that was the birthplace of the world's first operational cruise missile, the FZG 76. Hitler would soon refer to the missile as his vengeance weapon 1, or V-1.

The Army Research Center Peenemunde occupied the northeast corner of the island and ran down the eastern shore for about nine miles. A construction project that by August 1939 cost three hundred million reichsmarks would result in a series of large test stands on the northeast tip for the firing of massive rockets; a myriad of research, development, and production facilities; as well as an attractively designed village of steep-roofed row houses and well-appointed apartments to house the personnel working at both the Luftwaffe and army facilities. There were two new harbors built, a power plant, a sewage treatment plant, and a wind tunnel that eventually reached a speed of Mach 4.4, unheard of at the time. Everything had been built from the ground up. In many ways, Peenemunde was the forerunner of similar centers built at Oak Ridge, Tennessee, and Akademgordok in the Soviet Union. So many thousands of scientists, technicians, and others were employed at the Army Research Center that by 1942 its annual payroll reached nearly thirteen million reichsmarks. It was the birthplace of the rockets that would within a generation become intercontinental ballistic missiles and would take man into space.

By joint arrangement between the two services, the entire center was under army command. The Army Research Center, known as Peenemunde East, was placed under the direction of Wernher von Braun. By the summer of 1940, all rocket research was being done at Peenemunde, including that on a piloted rocket-powered Heinkel airplane, the He 112. But, the main thrust of the work done at Peenemunde East was on the rocket that eventually became known as the A4. Hitler called it his V-2.

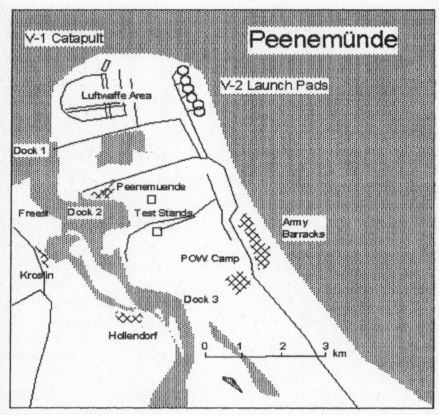

Map of Peenemunde, birthplace of the missile. *USED WITH PERMISSION OF MARK WADE, ENCYCLOPEDIA ASTRONAUTICA, WWW.ASTRONAUTIX.COM.*

## The Luftwaffe's V-1

The people of Great Britain, the first targets of these new weapons, called them Buzz Bombs and Doodlebugs because of the noise they made while in flight. The names belie the terror that noise created and the over five thousand people they killed and nearly sixteen thousand they wounded in a relatively short time near the end of the war.

The V-1 was actually a pilotless mid-wing aircraft that was launched from an extended ramp. It was twenty-four feet and four inches long and had a wingspan of seventeen feet, six inches. Once launched, it reached a height of approximately three thousand feet and a top speed of four hundred miles per hour. The pulse-jet engine mounted above the fuselage was timed to shut off at a preset distance from the launch site. The bomb would then tilt toward the target and hurtle to the earth, where its 1,870-pound warhead would explode on impact. At launch it weighed 4,806 pounds, which included 150 gallons of fuel. The standard range of the V-1 was about 150 miles.[6]

The first V-1 was launched from Peenemunde West on December 24, 1942, but it would be another seventeen months before they were ready for practical use. In comparison to the army's A4 rocket, with which it constantly competed for increasingly scarce resources and for Hitler's attention, the V-1 was simplicity itself. It was also relatively cheap to build compared to the rocket. Its biggest drawback was its speed. At 400 miles per hour, it was too slow to outrun Britain's best fighter defense forces. As a result, of the nearly ten thousand V-1s launched against Britain, nearly half were lost to defensive measures, including fighters, antiaircraft batteries, and barrage balloons. Allied fighter pilots shot down over six hundred over the English Channel alone.

The V-1 joined the war seven days after the Allies began landing in Normandy. During the night of June 13–14, 1944, Londoners were startled to hear the new, strange, shrill sound overhead, followed by explosions. Once the sound was identified for what it was, the suspense of waiting for the impact and explosion somewhere nearby was so great that Churchill wrote the V-1 attacks imposed on the people of London "a burden perhaps even heavier than the air raids of 1940 and 1941."[7]

According to the late highly respected British weaponry authority Ian Hogg, a German aerodynamicist named Paul Schmidt first devised the pulse-jet engine that drove the V-1 in the late 1920s. Schmidt used a combination of air pressure caused by the rush of air while in flight and a gasoline injection system to fuel the engine. The highly volatile combination was ignited periodically while in flight by a spark plug that received its power from a storage battery. The spark plug ignited the fuel several times each second, thus the term pulse-jet. The device was soon known as the Schmidt engine.

At first there seemed to be no real use for the Schmidt engine. This was because in order for the air pressure part of the fuel to function, the engine had to already have achieved a speed of at least 190 miles per hour. At lesser speeds the pressure was not great enough for the system to function properly. As a result, an aircraft that had to take off in the normal manner and speeds could not use it. The engine could not lift a plane off the ground or bring one in for a landing because it would shut down at low speed.

A second problem that prevented the Schmidt engine from being used to power a regular airplane was that the mechanical functions of the device began to deteriorate after about thirty to forty-five minutes of flight. This meant it was a one-way flight. Desperate to find a use for his invention, Schmidt suggested in 1934 that it might be used to power an aerial torpedo. At the time, no one seemed interested in that idea either.

Hogg reports that four years later the Air Ministry, which was reviewing various plans for jet engines, decided to have a Schmidt engine manufactured for further study of its potential use. The contract was given to the Argus Motor Works, which produced a pulse-jet engine with 661 pounds of thrust based on Schmidt's design. The Luftwaffe's specialists liked the engine, but still could not figure out what to do with it. Several test flights were made using the engine to power a manned aircraft. These included powering a glider after it became airborne, and as a second power source for a two-engine fighter. In the end these all proved disappointing.

Meanwhile, the air service's chief rival, the army, was experimenting with the development of missiles of its own. Perhaps fired by interservice rivalry, the Air Ministry put out a call for an airframe that would make use of the Schmidt engine and give the air force its own missile. By early 1942 Robert Lusser, an airframe specialist at the Fiesler aircraft company, submitted drawings of an airframe with the engine mounted above it. It was proposed that the weapon be fired from a long catapult. The Air Ministry liked the idea and on June 19, 1942, authorized its development. Argus and Fiesler entered into a joint partnership to build what they called the Fi 103, using Fiesler's regular project numbering system. The Luftwaffe renamed it the Flakzielgerat 76, a name that hid its true purpose and identified it as some sort of flying target for gunnery practice by antiaircraft crews. Its shortened name quickly became FZG 76.[8]

A major drawback to the V-1 was the 150-foot-long ramp that was required to get the craft moving fast enough so the pulse-jet engine would fire. The ramps were made in sections that could be locked together in advance of the firing. Without the ability to control the craft in flight, the ramp had to be set at an angle that fired the V-1 directly toward its target. The ramp was basically a long hollow tube with a slot in its top. A launch vehicle similar to a trolley sat on top of the tube and rested against a fin sticking up through the slot. The fin was part of a piston that when fired by the use of high-pressure steam, ran along the length of the inside of the tube pushing the trolley with it. The piston acted in the same manner as an artillery shell traveling along a gun barrel. The V-1 sat atop the trolley. When the piston was fired and the missile's engine started, the piston, trolley, and missile rocketed along the ramp until it reached the required speed. At the end of the ramp the piston and trolley fell away and the missile continued on its flight. The piston and trolley were retrieved for another firing. When the first ramps began to appear in Allied reconnaissance photos no one knew what they were to be used for, so they were periodically photographed until something happened.

Once the V-1 entered the war and the ramps were identified as the launcher sites, they were always targeted for bombing raids when they could be found. The Germans spent a tremendous amount of energy finding ways to camouflage them, something that proved extremely difficult considering their size and shape. The scientists worked on methods of decreasing the length of the launch platform by blasting increasingly larger amounts of compressed air at the missile in the seconds prior to launch to simulate flight and fire the engine earlier. If they had succeeded with this, they could have used considerably shorter launch ramps. Shortened ramps might have been mounted on ships or U-boats, which may be why Admiral Donitz was invited to view a firing of V-1s at Peenemunde on May 26, 1943.[9]

Several variations of the V-1 were developed, including a piloted model for use against attacking bomber fleets, and another using an improved engine design that extended the operational range to two hundred miles. A third type, used successfully in several raids against Britain, was launched from German bombers. The bomber favored for this service was the He 111.

Although there is no record of anyone in Germany thinking of the V-1 as a weapon for use against the United States, considering its limited range, it was something the American forces did regard as a possibility. The Germans ran out of time, but the Americans did not. Using several captured V-1s, the U.S. Navy found a way to launch them from submarines, and as we see later in this chapter, considered such an attack on the Japanese home islands.

## FROM BUZZ BOMBS TO LOONS

In an incredible demonstration of cooperation and coordination, a number of damaged components of V-1s that had been fired at British targets during the first month of their operation were recovered from crash sites. These were rushed to the United States. Within seventeen days of their arrival at Wright Field in Ohio in late July 1944, American engineers succeeded in using the components as guides to build and fire their own V-1 missile.

Over the next few months, American engineers continued working on the missile they had developed from the recovered V-1 components. Both the U.S. Air Corps and the U.S. Navy forged ahead with efforts to duplicate the V-1 to fit their needs during the remainder of the war. The Air Corps test-fired its version of the V-1, which they called the JB-2 (Jet Bomb-2), at Florida's Elgin Field (now Elgin Air Force Base) in October 1944, followed shortly by test firings at the Wendover Range in Utah (now the Utah Test and Training Range). The effort was then moved to New Mexico's Alamogordo Army Air Field (now Holloman Air Force Base) and Muroc Army Air Base (now Edwards Air Force Base) in California. Several of these facilities still have remains of the launch ramps built for the missile firings. Plans were soon begun to use these V-1s against the Japanese home islands. In order to rush their construction, contracts for as many as 2,000 JB-2s were issued. Launchers to be mounted beneath the wings of B-17G and B-29 bombers were developed. The Japanese surrender brought a halt to the construction of JB-2s after about one thousand had been completed, although work on guidance systems for the existing missiles continued after the war. The V-1/JB-2 "played a significant role in the development of surface to surface missile systems."[10]

The U.S. Navy took a different approach with the V-1. Also thinking about using the American V-1 missiles against Japanese targets, the navy wanted to know if they could be fired from a warship. The original plan was to build ramps on escort carriers that were intended for the fleet being assembled for the final campaign of the war, the invasion of Japan.[11]

The navy called its V-1 the KUW-1 Loon. Operating its V-1 project out of the facilities at the future Point Mugu Naval Air Missile Test Center in Ventura County, California, the navy hired Willy Fiedler to help supervise the work. Fiedler had been a designer and test pilot at Fiesler Aircraft Works before the war and had been transferred to Peenemunde to help build and test the V-1.[12]

The navy fired several dummy Loons from a beach-mounted ramp in early 1945. Impressed with the result, the Bureau of Aeronautics granted Republic Aviation a contract to build 151 Loons in June 1945. Following the Japanese surrender, the navy decided on a different approach to the use of the Loon, firing them from a submarine. This required reworking the launch method to allow for a much shorter ramp, one that could be mounted on the deck of a submarine. The method the navy settled on was a catapult fired by the explosion of black powder. This got the missile up to speed extremely quickly, thus allowing for the shorter ramp. The submarine selected for this task was the fleet boat USS *Cusk*.

Built by Electric Boat of Groton, Connecticut, the Balao Class submarine was commissioned on February 5, 1946. Soon after, she sailed for her home port of San Diego, where she was selected to become the first submarine to launch a guided missile. This "Mother of all Boomers" had a small hangar built on her deck just behind the sail, along with a short ramp. The Cusk made history on February 17, 1947, when she succeeded in firing the first Loon from her deck ramp. The missile she fired was

U.S. airmen preparing to fire a JB-2 missile in 1948. This was the Air Force ver-sion of the German V-1. *SPECIAL THANKS TO GEORGE MINDLING AND MARTYN D. TAGG.*

only slightly different from the one the Germans had fired at London. This one required a much-shortened ramp to reach the speed at which its pulse-jet engine would fire properly, was tracked by radar to its target, and was guided to that target by radio. The V-1 had become the world's first submarine-fired guided missile less than three years from the first time it entered the war. Given more time to develop the ability to fire a V-1 from the short ramp used by the U.S. Navy, there can be little doubt that the Germans would have used this weapon against cities along the East Coast of the United States.

The Loon was soon replaced by the Regulus, which itself was replaced by a long series of sub-launched guided missiles eventually leading to the nuclear powered Tomahawk missile and to sub-launched ballistic missiles such as Polaris, Poseidon, and Trident. The USS *Cusk* earned her place in history by firing the first submarine-launched guided missiles, both while on the surface and while submerged. That place was assured when she became the subject of a Hollywood movie called *The Flying Missile,* starring Glenn Ford.

Loon missile seconds before launch. U.S. Navy version of the German V-1. *OFFICIAL U.S. NAVY PHOTO PROVIDED BY NICK SPARK AND DAVID STUMPF.*

USS *Norton Sound* (AV-11) firing a Loon, the U.S. Navy's version of the German V-1. *U.S. NAVY PHOTO PROVIDED BY MATT CARRASCO OF WWW.USSNORTONSOUND.ORG.*

In the following chapter we examine a series of rocket firings from a submerged German U-boat that might have brought the submarine-fired guided missile into action a lot sooner. The technological problems could have been overcome, just as the U.S. Navy succeeded in doing, but the

USS *Carbonero* (SS-337) preparing to launch a Loon missile, the U.S. Navy copy of the German V-1. *U.S. NAVY PHOTO PROVIDED BY NICK SPARK AND DAVID STUMPF.*

biggest hurdle, the rivalry between the German Navy and the Luftwaffe, prevented the Germans from accomplishing the task.

We can only imagine what would have happened if the interservice rivalry had been set aside, and Admiral Donitz had been able to send a small group of U-boats to the United States' East Coast in late 1944 armed with V-1s that could be launched at the virtually unprotected cities of New York, Boston, and Washington, D.C.

## The Wehrmacht's V-2

Just as the V-1 was the precursor of the cruise missile, the V-2 was the forerunner of the intercontinental ballistic missile and the rockets that have sent men into space and taken them to the moon. The V-2 we are primarily concerned with is known as the A4 Rocket. This was the fourth-generation rocket designed and built by the team that came to occupy Peenemunde East. It was the first designed to meet military specifications that included a payload that could be a warhead.

Work began on the A1 rocket in 1933. Less than five feet long, it provided the designers, including the ever-present Dornberger, whose job it was to constantly find the funds required to keep the project going as well as expand it, with a long list of technical difficulties that had to be overcome. The A1 was never actually tested in flight. Before that could happen, the changes required to achieve success led to the A2 in 1934. A few days before Christmas 1934, two A2 rockets were success fully

Cover of Chrysler Corporation brochure for a display of V-2 missiles at the Michigan State Fair in 1953. *COURTESY OF DAIMLERCHRYSLER CORPORATION.*

fired. The rockets had been nicknamed Max and Moritz, after two popular comic strip characters. The two were also well known in the United States as Hans and Fritz, trouble-prone boys in the comic strip called *The Katzenjammer Kids.* Fired from an island in the Baltic Sea, both rockets reached an altitude of 1.4 miles. It was an auspicious beginning to the

Captured German V-2 rocket being prepared for firing aboard the U.S. Navy aircraft carrier *Midway* during Operation Sandy on September 6, 1947. *OFFICIAL U.S.
NAVY PHOTO COURTESY OF EVAN NAU.*

program that would ultimately lead to rockets powerful enough to take
tons of payloads, including men, into space.[13]

Next in line came the A3, which was a quantum leap for the rocket
men of Germany. This vehicle was over 21 feet long and nearly two and
one-half feet in diameter. It was equipped with three gyroscopes and two
integrating accelerometers for guidance, and the latest and most sophisti-
cated control systems. Three A3s were launched in the fall of 1937. While
the launches themselves were successful, the guidance and control systems
did not perform as well as they had in the laboratory and the engineers had
to rethink some of their assumptions concerning the vehicles' design.[14]

There was also the question of payload, since this was intended as a
weapon of war. They eventually arrived at the conclusion that the rocket
that would meet their goals had to be much larger than the A3, both in

Wernher von Braun and others boarding the USS *Midway* for Operation Sandy.
*OFFICIAL U.S. NAVY PHOTO COURTESY OF WILLIAM BEGGS, JR.*

length and width, and would have to carry a payload of about one metric ton. Dornberger, thinking ahead about the need to transport the rockets to various launch locations, placed limits on its size. It would have to be moved by both road and rail, so it could not be wider than the maximum width of the trucks and trailers then available, and it would have to be able to pass through any railroad tunnel in Germany. The result was the next big step, the A4.[15]

The A4 was the world's first ballistic missile. It was 46 feet long and had a diameter of 5 feet 5 inches. It had four fins at the rear or bottom of the body with a span of 11 feet, 8 inches. Prior to fueling it weighed 8,818 pounds, including a warhead usually containing 1,654 pounds of conventional high explosives. Fully fueled for launch it weighed 28,440 pounds.

Captured German V-2 rocket parked on a street in Alamogordo, New Mexico, 1946. *USED WITH PERMISSION AND THANKS TO WILLIAM BEGGS, JR.*

Its fuel was a mixture of alcohol and liquid oxygen that it consumed at a rate of 280 pounds per second when fired. It took the A4 approximately sixty-five seconds to consume its fuel, by which time it was moving faster than the speed of sound and had tilted toward its target, which in its latter stages of development could be as far as 220 miles away.

The first A4 was launched on June 13, 1942, from Test Stand 7 at Peenemunde. With a large group of excited engineers, technicians, and others watching, the rocket slowly lifted off its launch platform and rose into the dense clouds above the onlookers. For a few moments it appeared this first actual launch of the giant rocket would achieve its goal, but all hearts stopped momentarily when a loud rumble was heard within the clouds and the rocket suddenly reappeared as it tumbled end over end into the Baltic only a short distance away. Despite this failure, a second launch was made on August 16. This launch was only slightly more successful. The rocket rose into a clear summer sky, reaching an altitude of about five miles when the nose suddenly broke off. It too ended up sinking into the Baltic.

Finally, on October 3, 1942, the first successful launch of an A4 was accomplished. This time the rocket reached an altitude in excess of fifty miles and a range of 120 miles. This was followed by an aggressive program of development and experimentation that led, in September 1944, to the first use of the rockets as weapons of war. The first two were fired at Paris on September 6. Within days, rocket attacks were launched against London and Antwerp; the latter Belgian port was being used by the Allies to supply the forces that had landed since D-Day.

By war's end the Germans are believed to have built over five thousand V-2 rockets, of which slightly more than one thousand reached targets in England. Later models made use of enhancements in targeting and range, but it all proved too late to impact the outcome of the war.

## Making a Missile Intercontinental

The A4 rocket was satisfactory for its original goal of delivering a warhead to a target located a maximum of 220 miles from the launch point. In order to increase the rocket's range, development began on the A9, a winged version of the V-2. Adding wings meant that the rocket, once it reached its peak altitude and the fuel was exhausted, would not merely turn and plummet toward the earth. The wings would, in the words of famed rocket expert Willy Ley, make the vessel operate as a "high-speed glider."[16]

Turning the rocket into a glider, and thus consuming much of its return-to-earth speed in a long gradual decline in altitude would solve another problem with the A4. When the missile came virtually straight down, its own speed would drive it into the ground before it exploded, thus much of the explosion would be absorbed by the earth around it. If it hit its target in a slow glide, it might then explode as it struck the earth, causing more widespread death and destruction.

As conceived, the A9 was very similar in length and dimensions to the A4. It appears that the idea of adding wings to an enhanced A4 rocket in order to extend its range originated with a designer named Kurt Patt. Patt proposed using the A4's engine to power a flying wing that had no actual fuselage. The idea itself proved too radical for the men working on the A4, but they liked the use of wings and adapted the idea to their

Scale model of the manned version of the A9 intercontinental missile. This award-winning model was built and photographed by Richard Benavides. *USED WITH HIS PERMISSION.*

rocket. They estimated that they could double a standard-shaped rocket's range with the addition of wings.[17]

The project was never one of high priority, so the development of a winged A4 was constantly on a back burner, until Allied forces landed in Normandy and began the process of driving the German Army out of Western Europe, eventually putting London beyond the range of the A4. By the summer of 1944 the decision was made to put the A9 into production despite the fact that research on an improved propulsion system had not been completed. Instead of a new rocket, the A9 would be basically the A4 with wings attached. Hitler was still clinging to the idea that he could force Great Britain out of the war if he could terrorize the British population with massive attacks on London and other nearby cities.[18]

After the war, Dornberger wrote that the development of the winged rocket, the A9, "did not satisfy our ambitions." What they wanted to build, he wrote, was a rocket that would "cover thousands of miles," not simply hundreds.[19]

Had they succeeded in building a rocket that could "cover thousands of miles," the obvious target was the United States, as it was the only major Allied enemy power that was thousands of miles from German territory. It can safely be assumed from Dornberger's postwar comment that their "ambitions" were to launch such a long-range missile against targets on the American mainland.

As early as July 1941, Dornberger prepared a memorandum for Hitler under the direction of the army Commander-in-Chief Field Marshal Walther von Brauchitsch emphasizing the importance of the rocket program to German morale. Dornberger also discussed the development of a two-stage missile that would be capable of reaching targets in the United States.[20]

The Smithsonian Institution's Michael J. Neufeld reports that work on the design for a two-stage missile, dubbed the "America Rocket," had actually begun at Peenemunde's Projects Office a year earlier. According to Neufeld, scientists working under the direction of Ludwig Roth had already been looking into the possibility of placing an A9 on top of a huge booster rocket designated the A10. The concept appealed to von Braun and his engineers, but it was, as Neufeld writes, "beyond Peenemunde's grasp."[21]

Dornberger called the two-stage rocket a "better plan" for launching the long-range A9 than the alternative being investigated, which was a catapult that had been designed using the launching ramps of the V-1 as a guide. Mounting the A9 on top of a booster rocket permitted both to be launched from a vertical position, reducing the need to build large installations that could be more easily targeted by Allied bombers. Dornberger explained that the A10 had a thrust of 200 tons for fifty to sixty seconds, enough to lift the A9 to an altitude of nearly 35 miles and a speed of 2,700 miles per hour. After consuming all its fuel, the parachute-equipped A10 would be dead weight that would only slow down the warhead-equipped missile atop it, so it would then drop away and fall into the sea, where it would be recovered for future use. The A9 would then turn toward its far-off target, fire its own power plant to increase its speed, and achieve the required range. Dornberger estimated that the A9 could "cover 2,500 miles in about 35 minutes." When its own fuel was exhausted, the A9 would gradually slow and begin its return to earth in a long hypersonic glide to its target.[22]

On August 20, 1941, Dornberger, von Braun, and Ernst Steinhoff, head of guidance development, met with Hitler at the Fuhrer's East Prussia headquarters known as the "Wolf's Lair." They showed Hitler films of various rocket launchings, and Dornberger spoke at length about the various projects they were developing, including the two-stage rocket. In a letter written the following month to Armaments Minister Fritz Todt, in which he described the meeting with Hitler, Dornberger emphasized the importance of continued development of long-range rockets "if we want to beat the Americans."[23]

In his memoir, Dornberger discussed the development of rocket-driven aircraft, which most likely was the piloted version of the A9 then under development, mounted atop an A10 booster rocket. His goal was to build a craft that was capable of flying from "Europe to America in 40 minutes."[24]

The piloted version of the A9 was bandied about for quite a while. It offered the opportunity to overcome the serious and unresolved issues of guiding the missile to its target. Guidance systems were not yet advanced to the stage that a missile that reached the United States could, with any hope of success, be aimed at a targeted city. With a pilot aboard the A9, the missile could come within sight of a landmark; the Empire State Building was one often used. Once he had the building in sight, the pilot could aim his craft at it, and eject. His fate would be to either become a prisoner of war, or if lucky, be rescued by a U-boat standing by waiting for him. Although this concept lasted for a while and garnered some support, it never reached a stage of development that might produce such a craft.

Early in 1944, further work on the development of the A10 booster rocket was halted when it was determined that it would require at least two more years of work before the rocket could be employed. A few months later work on an improved propulsion system for the A9 was stopped and a decision made to prepare a winged rocket for immediate use against the Allies. The rocket's designation was changed to the A4b. In order to make quick use of the wing-extended range idea, it was decided that the A4b should be built using only parts and assemblies identical to those of the A4. This would speed up its production and deployment.[25]

The first winged A9/A4b was launched on January 8, 1945. A failure in its electrical control system caused the rocket to fall back to earth after reaching an altitude of only one hundred feet. A much more successful launch took place on January 24. This time the A9/A4b reached an altitude of fifty miles and a speed of 2,700 miles per hour, but time was running out for the scientists and engineers. The Soviet Army had already reached the Oder, and everyone recognized that the end was approaching rapidly. As a result, Peenemunde was soon evacuated.[26]

The combined A9 and A10, had there been more time and additional materials available, would have been Nazi Germany's intercontinental ballistic missile. Neufeld estimated that had the work been completed it would have been "only marginally able to reach East Coast cities."

After the war, Wernher von Braun told American interrogators that his engineers had conducted preliminary design studies on an A11. This was a booster rocket on which the A9/A10 combination would be mounted for launch. They calculated that through the use of a three-stage rocket system they could get the A9 into orbital powerless flight, thus extending its range to anywhere on the earth.[27]

As with so many other weapons intended for attack against the American mainland, time and material ran out on the Nazi ICBM before the goal could be achieved.

## AMERICA ROCKETS AT THE DEATH FACTORY

The evil eminence of Heinrich Himmler began to cast a shadow over the German rocket program at the end of 1942. Until October of that year Hitler had been supportive but skeptical of the rocket program. It appears he was never really comfortable with technological advances that went beyond the technology of the First World War. On October 14, 1942, the Fuhrer had a change of heart after Minister of Armaments Albert Speer told him that an A4 had successfully been launched and had flown 120 miles and struck within two and one-half miles of its target. Perhaps it was this apparent success, combined with the bad news of the impending disaster at Stalingrad, that prompted Hitler to look with increased hope at this new weapon. In any case, Speer reported that Hitler insisted that the A4 go into mass production immediately and that five thousand of them be "available for wholesale commitment."[28]

Hitler's newfound interest in the rockets must have ignited Himmler's natural inclination to bring everything significant in Germany under the control of his SS empire. On December 11 Himmler made his first tour of Peenemunde. While there, he witnessed the launch of an A4. Despite the fact that this launch was a complete failure, the Reichsfuhrer-SS began taking steps to bring the entire operation under his control.[29]

Along with SS influence and eventual control over the rocket program came the introduction of slave labor to increase production. The drastic shortage of skilled German labor was being met in a number of industries by the use first of Soviet POWs, but soon also by concentration camp internees. Through its Economic and Administrative Main Office, the SS had established what Michael J. Neufeld called a "rent-a-slave service." The first of these to be used in production related to the rocket program was early in 1943, when camp inmates were assigned to work at the Zeppelin facilities manufacturing various A4 components including fuselage sections and propellant tanks. In mid-June the first SS prisoners began arriving at Peenemunde to work on the actual assembly of rockets.[30]

On the night of August 17, 1943, based on a number of intelligence reports concerning the work being done at Peenemunde on both the V-1 and V-2 weapons, the facility was targeted for what became a devastating raid. Nearly six hundred British Stirling, Lancaster, and Halifax bombers carried out Operation Hydra. German fighters had been successfully lured away from the target by a diversionary raid on Berlin by eight Mosquito light bombers. As a result of Operation Hydra, 130 German scientists, engineers, and technicians were killed, including Dr. Walter Thiel, designer of the A4 propulsion system. Also killed were about six hundred foreign workers, mostly POWs and concentration camp inmates.[31]

As a result of this raid, the decision was made to relocate rocket production to a site safer from Allied bombers. Anxious to find a way to gain control over the rocket program, Himmler suggested to Hitler that the production facilities for the A4 be moved underground, where Allied bombs could not reach them. He also told Hitler that he believed spies had been responsible for betraying Peenemunde as the home of the rocket development work. Himmler's answer to this was to employ forced labor from his concentration camps, along with skilled German workers from his prisons, for the assembly of all rockets. Hitler responded enthusiastically to the proposal, and Himmler quickly made his move. On August 21 he wrote to Minister of Armaments Albert Speer that "in my capacity as Reichsfuhrer-SS, I am taking over the production of the A4 device...." He then appointed a reliable SS officer, Brigadier General Dr. Hans Kammler, to construct the new secret underground assembly plants for the A4.[32]

A product of a middle-class upbringing, Kammler was by all outward appearances the perfect Nazi type. Tall, blue-eyed, with blond hair, always impeccably dressed, he was a university-educated architect and civil engineer. He was also as ruthless, overbearing, and arrogant as his boss. A member of Himmler's inner circle, Kammler had played a significant part in the design and construction of the gas chambers and extermination camps at Auschwitz-Birkenau, Belzec, and Maidenek.[33]

The place chosen by Kammler for the serial production of the A4 and several other secret weapons was in a vast tunnel complex deep in the Hartz Mountains near the town of Nordhausen. A similar facility near the village of Ebensee in the Salzkammergut area of Upper Austria was to house new research operations. Both locations were to make use of slave labor from concentration camps for construction—and any other uses to which these poor people could be put.

Inmates from the notorious Austrian concentration camp at Mauthausen were transferred to a satellite camp near Ebensee in November 1943 to begin tunneling work. By April 1945 nearly nineteen thousand inmates were housed in the small camp. Thousands died from starvation, overwork, and abuse by their SS overlords. It was here that research and development work was to take place on two super-secret projects. They were *Wasserfall* (Waterfall), a ground-to-air missile system, and *Amerikarakette* (America Rocket), the two-stage intercontinental missile based on the A9/A10 concept. As work on the tunnels neared completion, the need for fuel overrode the need for advanced weapons. As a result, further research on the America Rocket and Waterfall were cancelled near the end of 1944, and a crude oil refinery was put into place instead.[34]

At Nordhausen, which operated under the name Mittelwerke (Central Works), thousands more inmates from Buchenwald Concentration Camp worked and died in horrible conditions to build several thousand A4 rockets. One report claims that as many as sixty thousand inmates were sent there to work, and twenty thousand perished. The German dream of launching rockets into outer space, where they would effortlessly circle the earth, ended in a dark, damp cavern full of human misery.[35]

For some, the question remains: Were the Germans trying to build a rocket that could reach the United States? The answer comes from one of those slave laborers. Alex Baum was a member of the French resistance when the Germans captured him. He was sent to Peenemunde and then to Mittelwerke. At both locations he worked on the V-2 program. Baum, who was born in a region close to the German border and had a good understanding of the German language, recalls overhearing a conversation between von Braun and Himmler, in which the scientist told the Nazi mass murderer about "the ultimate weapon that's going to destroy the United States and everything else."[36]

## MISSION APHRODITE

On April 12, 1943, the vice chiefs of the British Imperial General Staff met to discuss a report titled "German Long Range Rocket Development." In the previous four months they had received no less than five reports claiming the Germans were working on the development of long-range rockets. As a result of this, and of a secret meeting with Prime Minister Winston Churchill, Churchill's son-in-law, Duncan Sandys, was assigned the job of determining the truth to these reports. A member of the House of Commons with widespread connections in both the intelligence and scientific communities, a veteran of the Norway Campaign, and former commander of the first experimental rocket regiment, Sandys was well suited for the post.[37]

Simultaneously, the Director of Intelligence (Science) of the Air Staff, Reginald V. Jones, was also investigating the possibility that the Germans were developing long-range missiles of some type. Jones had earned a doctorate for research in infrared radiation from Oxford, and was as well connected as Sandys.[38]

One result of these two investigations was that a huge amount of information from a wide variety of sources began arriving concerning the German work being done on the pilotless aircraft now known as the V-1 and the V-2 rockets. Much of this information pointed toward Usedom Island on the Baltic coast as the center of research and development for these new weapons. Operation Hydra, the night bombing raid on Peenemunde, was a result of analysis of photographs taken during reconnaissance missions flown over the area. The photos revealed the presence of both the V-1 and the V-2 at the sites.

Another result was the discovery of seven sites along the French Channel coast at which extremely large-scale concrete construction was under way. Allied photo analysts could not clearly identify what the Germans were building, but most felt sure the sites were somehow related to the German secret weapons program. They were correct. Of the seven sites they found, two were intended for the launchings of A4 rockets, one was planned for a high-pressure gun that was never completed, and four were to be used for storing and launching V-1s against England. When these sites proved to be resistant to conventional bombing, the U.S. Army Air Corps came up with what it hoped would be the solution. In a super-secret operation code-named Aphrodite, several B-24s and B-17s were stripped of all equipment not absolutely essential to flying. The planes were then packed with high explosives. The plan was to put two men aboard a flying bomb to get it off the ground and headed in the right direction. At a predetermined location, control of the aircraft would be turned over to a second bomber through radio control and the two men would parachute to safety. The manned bomber, called the "mother" plane, would then guide the drone, called the "baby" by the men involved in the program. As they approached the target, the baby would be aimed directly at the large doors marking the entrance to the concrete bunker, in the hope it would impact directly at the doors and explode inside the structure. It proved to be a highly dangerous operation that cost the lives of many men, including Lieutenant Joseph P. Kennedy Jr., brother of the future president.[39]

Rumors and reports circulated that the Germans were working on a rocket that could reach New York, and it was to be launched from one of these bunkers. In his history of Aphrodite, Jack Olsen reports that "midnight telephone calls were flying back and forth and jump pilots (the men who piloted the drones) hastily recruited and the menace to New York and London and even Pittsburgh discussed till all hours of the morning by the highest ranking Allied officers."[40]

Even after the war, the reports of a German attempt to build an intercontinental missile continued. A postwar study issued by the U.S. Navy Technical Mission on Guided Missiles referred to the planned development of the A9/A10 two-stage rocket system as intended for use against the United States in the early months of 1946. It then claimed this two-stage rocket was "scientifically possible and undoubtedly would have been realized had time permitted."[41]

The Germans never put the concrete bunker sites to their planned use. When Allied infantry overran them, it was obvious that no rockets or other craft had ever been stored or launched from them. But until then, they had Allied planners worried over their true purpose. One especially concerned the Americans, the bunker located at Wizernes. While the others all appeared to be facing, and thus aimed, at either London or Bristol, this one was different. Alarms went off in early 1944 when a photo interpreter discovered that this bunker was aimed "within a half degree of the accurate Great Circle bearing on New York." The reason for this has never been explained. Also left unexplained is why the bombproof doors for this particular bunker were twice the size needed to pass an A4 through them. We are left to speculate whether this was to be the launch site for the combined A9/A10 intercontinental missile that many Germans hoped would bring the war home to America.[42]

## From Peenemunde to Midway

The first A4 rocket was successfully launched from Peenemunde on October 3, 1942. Less than five years later, on September 6, 1947, the

U.S. Navy did something the Germans would have envied: the firing of an A4 from the deck of a ship at sea.

Following the German surrender, American forces accepted the surrender of several hundred Peenemunde scientists and engineers and their families. Von Braun and Dornberger had made the decision to flee toward the American forces with the hope they would be better treated by the Americans than by the Soviets, and that the American government might allow them to continue their research and development on rockets. They were correct on both accounts.

The Germans revealed to their captors that the Nordhausen production facility contained a large number of completed and partially completed rockets, as well as thousands of parts for additional A4s. They also led them to a mineshaft in which they had hidden several tons of documents relating to their rocketry research. Unfortunately, both locations were within what would soon be the Soviet zone of occupation. Anxious to get everything they could to the United States before the Soviets or even the British realized what had happened, a twenty-six-year-old New Yorker with a degree in physics, Major James P. Hamill, was given the secret assignment to recover every valuable rocket part he could and get them to Antwerp, where they would be put aboard Liberty ships. Hamill and his team overcame monumental obstacles to gather up and move over 340 rail cars of V-2 components out of the tunnel complex while fending off Soviet intelligence officers who were also looking for the rockets. The last train departed one day before the Soviets were to officially take control of the area. The quick action and ingenuity of men such as Hamill, Major William Bromley, Colonel Gervais William Trichel, and Colonel Holger Toftoy laid the groundwork for the U.S. rocket program that eventually put an American on the moon. Theirs is a remarkable story of personal courage and rule-bending that is too often overlooked in the history of American space travel.[43]

The Liberty ships carrying the V-2 components arrived in New Orleans and were transferred to railroad cars for shipment to the White Sands Proving Grounds in New Mexico. Contemporary reports indicate that every railroad siding from El Paso, Texas, to Belen, New Mexico, was crammed with rail cars under army control. It took about twenty days to unload the rail cars, transfer the cargo to flatbed trucks, and deliver the V-2 material to the Proving Grounds. Soon after, the army began test firing its German rockets.

The firing we are most concerned with was done to determine if a rocket could successfully be launched from a moving platform such as a ship at sea. Naval officials also wanted to be sure that once a rocket was fired from the deck of an aircraft carrier, the deck would not suffer any damage and could quickly be used for aircraft takeoffs. The aircraft carrier USS *Midway* was under way on September 6, 1947, not far from Bermuda, when the A4 was fueled and prepared for launching from the flight deck. The launch took place without a hitch and the carrier's aircraft immediately used the deck for takeoff.[44]

Although there is no hard evidence that anyone of significance in the rocket program in Nazi Germany gave serious thought to launching V-2s from the decks of ships, it is interesting to note how closely this event followed the German surrender. It is certainly food for thought to the entire "What if" industry that has grown up around the history of the Second World War.

# CHAPTER 6

# U-Boats to America

WHILE THE LUFTWAFFE WAS OCCUPIED TRYING TO BUILD A BOMBER capable of reaching the United States, and the Wehrmacht was busy attempting to develop an intercontinental missile, the Kriegsmarine—German Navy—was determined to participate in the quest to bring the war to American cities.

Despite the early high hopes of many naval officials that Hitler would make the investment required to build a world-class navy for Germany so she would be equipped to fight a world-class naval power like the United States, it never happened. The aircraft carriers and fleet of battleships they dreamed of were never to be. The navy had to satisfy itself that it was little more than a commerce raiding force centered on a submarine fleet. The money was spent on building Germany's might to fight a large-scale land war instead.

In one of his histories of the war, Gerhard L. Weinberg discusses what he calls "a sort of underwater Pearl Harbor." This was a study that Hitler ordered in either late 1940 or early 1941, before the United States entered the war. Its genesis was a submarine attack against an American fleet while it was at anchor in a home port. The final report of the study was issued on March 22, 1941. It concluded that U-boats would not be able to success-fully enter U.S. naval anchorages without being detected because of their strong defenses, especially the heavy reliance on antisubmarine nets.[1]

If we think about the genuine Pearl Harbor, it is clear that the success of Japan's attack was primarily because of the powerful carrier-based navy she had built, along with a strong naval air arm. Neither of these factors ever existed for Nazi Germany. The closest Germany came to building an aircraft carrier was the on-and-off-again construction program on the Graf Zeppelin, which never approached completion, and for which only a few aircraft were ever developed.[2]

Perhaps lending credence to the German concern over antisubmarine measures is the fact that the only portion of the Japanese attack on Pearl Harbor that failed was the attempt to penetrate the American anchorage by five of Japan's midget submarines. All were lost during the attack, and a sailor from one of them became the first Japanese prisoner of war.[3]

Hitler wasn't alone in considering a German U-boat attack against the American mainland before the United States joined the Allies in the war. In mid-March 1941, the U.S. Navy's intelligence agency, the Office of Naval Intelligence, activated two sections to deal with issues related to German activities. The Coastal Information Section was charged with watching Atlantic coastal waters for German submarines. Information collected was to be passed on to navy destroyers on patrol and army air patrols. The Commerce and Travel Section "worked with other government offices to check visas, search for possible suspicious persons aboard ships in U.S. ports—especially Axis radio operators—and to detect sabotage."[4]

The entire issue of defending against potential attacks or sabotage faltered in the summer of 1941 in a quagmire of interagency rivalries and turf protection, just as it apparently did in the summer of 2001. President Roosevelt attempted to bring some order to the mass of agencies collecting information on June 18, 1941, when he appointed William J. "Wild Bill" Donovan as Coordinator of Information. Donovan's responsibility was "to collect and analyze all information bearing on national security, to 'correlate such information and data,' and to make it available to the President."[5]

Despite Donovan's direct access to the President, the new office he formed was "formidably opposed by J. Edgar Hoover, Director of the Federal Bureau of Investigation, the army's military intelligence organization (Military Intelligence Division), and the Office of Naval Intelligence."[6]

The Military Intelligence Division and the Office of Naval Intelligence considered Donovan's Office of Coordinator of Information "an unwelcome rival in the intelligence field." The MID and the ONI both prepared intelligence summaries that were presented to Roosevelt and key cabinet officers on alternating days. They both feared that Donovan's new group would supersede them when it came to winning the President's attention on intelligence matters. A plan was briefly considered to combine the army and navy agencies with Donovan's office so "the two service organizations could watch and outvote the civilian intelligence agency." Captain Alan Kirk, the Director of Naval Intelligence, decided against this, "opting instead for complete ONI autonomy and limiting contact with other bureaus through liaison officers and committees."[7]

The Japanese attack on Pearl Harbor on December 7, 1941, surprised the Germans as much as it did the Americans. For months Hitler and his foreign service henchmen had been urging Japan to take definitive action against Great Britain's interests in the Pacific and against the United States. Noted military historian and biographer Clay Blair reports that when it finally happened, when the Japanese attacked the United States at Pearl Harbor and British forces in Malaya, Hitler was "embarrassed and angry that the Japanese had not taken him into their confidence." Hitler considered himself the senior member of the Germany, Italy, Japan Axis; now the Japanese had gone out on their own without informing him of their plans, much less asking for his advice or assistance.[8]

Despite the perceived insult from his ally, and the fact that the Soviets had themselves just launched a surprise counteroffensive, sending one hundred fresh divisions against the German lines facing Moscow that appeared to be headed toward a Soviet breakthrough, Hitler turned his attention to the enemy he was about to make. He prepared a directive instructing the army to stand fast against the Soviet onslaught, and left his East Prussian headquarters to rush back to Berlin so he could publicly declare war against the United States.[9]

Hitler biographer Alan Bullock identified three factors that he credited with affecting Hitler's decision to declare war on the United States, even as his army was facing a potential disaster on the Eastern Front and the last thing Germany needed was another powerful enemy. One was Hitler's resentment over the secret war President Roosevelt had been conducting at sea against German submarines; another was his vision of the entire world being impacted by the decision. Perhaps the most important was "his disastrous underestimate of American strength."[10]

At his war crimes trial at Nuremberg, Hitler's Foreign Minister Joachim von Ribbentrop claimed he attempted to dissuade the Fuhrer from his planned declaration of war. He related how he pointed out to Hitler that the Tripartite Pact on which the Axis of Germany, Italy, and Japan was built required Germany to come to Japan's aid only if she was attacked. Obviously, in this case, Japan was the attacker, which did not require action on Germany's part. Hitler, he said, brushed this objection aside with the comment that the United States had already been at war with Germany since her navy had been firing at German ships; and besides, if Germany did not now stand with Japan, "the Pact is politically dead."[11]

Not everyone is convinced by von Ribbentrop's statement that he tried to prevent the declaration. Gerhard L. Weinberg writes, "Unlike all other major policy choices of the regime, however, this was one on which there appear to have been no oral or written dissents." He continues, "There is a curious irony in a situation where the leaders of a country were united on a war with the one nation they were least likely and worst equipped to defeat."[12]

Perhaps they were united because they were all still convinced that the United States was a mongrel nation incapable of fighting a war against such a great power as the Third Reich had become under Adolf Hitler. At his headquarters in the occupied French Atlantic port of Lorient, Admiral Karl Donitz, commander of Hitler's U-boat fleets, read the reports of the attack on Pearl Harbor at about the same time Hitler did. On his world globe he measured the course from Lorient to New York City and determined which of his submarines were capable of reaching the American coast and remaining there long enough to strike a serious blow at the Americans before they could build up their defenses.[13]

Even in 1945, as the war appeared to be winding down, the fear of an attack on American cities was real. A contemporary observer could justify those fears by simply recalling events since the attack on Pearl Harbor. On February 23, 1942, a Japanese submarine, I-17, entered the Santa Barbara Strait undetected while submerged. At about 5:40 p.m. she surfaced and proceeded to fire seventeen shells into the oil storage facility at Ellwood City. The following day California newspaper headlines screamed about the attack by a "Jap U-Boat" and demanded increased security measures along the coast. Radio Tokyo made the most of the small attack, calling it a warning that "the paradise created by George Washington is on the verge of destruction."[14]

On June 20 of the same year a Japanese submarine shelled a radio transmitter station on Vancouver Island. The following day another Japanese sub, I-25, shelled a military depot at Fort Stevens on Oregon's Columbia River.[15]

On September 9, 1942, the I-25 launched its *Glen* reconnaissance seaplane from a position within sight of the Cape Blanco lighthouse on the Oregon coast. Piloted by Warrant Flying Officer Nobuo Fujita and Petty Officer Shoji Okuda, the single-engine aircraft flew some fifty miles inland and dropped two 167-pound incendiary bombs into the heavily wooded Oregon interior in an attempt to start large-scale forest fires. A second, similar mission was conducted on September 29. Although the bombs did result in small fires that were extinguished by forest rangers, the larger goal of starting massive fires failed due to heavy rains that had soaked the forests for several days before each raid. A wartime ban on broadcasting weather information along the coast helped to avoid warning the Japanese that the forests were probably too wet to burn. Rangers recovered sixty-five pounds of metal fragments and thermite pellets from the first raid that were clearly identified as Japanese. We can only wonder what the result would have been if it were not for the rain, or if the bombs had been dropped on a populated area. Despite government attempts to keep the raids secret, word of them reached local newspapers and caused a public demand for additional defense of the coastal area.[16]

Although German U-boats had not actually attacked targets on the U.S. mainland, they had successfully mined the waters around important mainland ports from Jacksonville, Florida, to Boston. On at least two occasions U-boats had surfaced and shelled oil storage facilities on Aruba and at Curacao. The danger of a U-boat attack on a major American city remained a reality right up until the end of the war.[17]

By early 1945, Allied intelligence had learned much about the advanced weapons the Germans were developing. This knowledge added to the fear of an attack by them making use of their deadly submarines. In January 1945, *The New York Times* summed up that fear in a news story titled "Bombing the Atlantic Coast." The article began quite ominously, "Last November the Army and Navy jointly stated that attacks on this country by V-1 or V-2 bombs are entirely possible. It was assumed that the bombs would be launched not from Europe but from submarines lying off our shore, from long-range planes which would make a one-way 'sacrifice flight' and which would be controlled across the Atlantic by submarines or by catapult plane tenders." After discussing the limited amount of damage such an attack might cause in comparison to the result of the V-1 and V-2 attacks on London, the piece concluded with the warning that "it is just as well to assume that an attack may be made. . . ."[18]

## DRUMBEAT AND PASTORIUS

Hitler was so anxious to begin his war with America that two days before his war declaration speech to a cheering meeting of Reichstag Deputies on December 11, 1941, he met with Admiral Erich Raeder, commander-in-chief of the German Navy. He told Raeder to unleash Donitz's U-boats against American ships and to plan attacks along the United States' East Coast. Raeder quickly passed the Fuhrer's instructions on to Donitz, who made the following entry in his war diary for December 9, 1941: ". . . the whole area of the American coasts will become open for operations by U-boats. . . ." In this way began a project that Donitz called Operation Paukenschlag (Drumbeat).[19]

Operation Drumbeat was arguably one of the most successful operations of the German Navy during the war. Its goal was to cut off the vital lifeline between the United States and Great Britain. Without the steady shipment of food and military supplies from the United States, the Germans were convinced, and with justification, that England could not hold out against the Nazi onslaught. Although the operation did not sever the lifeline completely, it did severely reduce the quantity of supplies being shipped to a beleaguered England for a time. The impact of Operation

Drumbeat in just the first half of 1942 was expressed by Army Chief of Staff General George C. Marshall in a June 19, 1942, memorandum: "The losses by submarines off our Atlantic seaboard and in the Caribbean now threaten our entire war effort."[20]

A U.S. Navy manual expressed it in similar language: "The massacre enjoyed by the U-boats along our Atlantic Coast in 1942 was as much a national disaster as if saboteurs had destroyed half a dozen of our biggest war plants."[21]

Starting in January 1942, U-boats operated off the American East Coast with almost total impunity. They were aided by the ineffectiveness of civilian and naval crews with little or no experience or training in combating submarines, and the prolonged refusal of many coastal areas to black out their lights at night. German skippers had only to sit offshore and pick off their targets as well-lit towns and resorts silhouetted the ships against the ocean darkness. In January some forty-six Allied ships were sunk off the coast. The following month sixty-five were sent to the bottom of the ocean.[22]

Not until April did an American destroyer sink the first U-boat in American waters. The aged destroyer USS *Roper*, under the command of Lieutenant Commander Hamilton W. Howe, made this first kill off the coast of North Carolina. The *Roper* was from the U.S. Navy's Fifth Naval District, with headquarters in Norfolk, Virginia. Said to be the best trained of the navy's antisubmarine forces along the East Coast, the district had declared an aggressive "hunter-killer" policy on April 1, in which its entire complement of surface vessels and aircraft maintained intensive ocean patrols in search of the German sub force.[23]

Shortly after midnight on April 14, the *Roper*'s radar picked up a blip that was soon identified as a surfaced submarine. The speedier destroyer chased the blip down, avoiding a torpedo fired from the pursued U-boat, which was later identified as U-85 commanded by Lieutenant Eberhard Greger. When the *Roper* came within three hundred yards of the submarine, Howe turned on his ship's twenty-four-inch searchlight and opened fire on her with his Number 1 machine, followed by a well-placed shell from the *Roper*'s three-inch gun. The shell slammed into U-85's conning tower and she began almost immediately to go down. Howe then ordered a depth charge barrage to ensure the sub did not surface again. The following morning, twenty-nine bodies of German submariners were fished from the sea. It was the first time the navy's Eastern Seaboard Frontier defense system had a reason to celebrate.[24]

Admiral Donitz's U-boat force participated in an even more daring and potentially more lethal operation against the United States the following year—the landing of saboteurs at two locations on the American mainland.

It was called Operation Pastorius. Planned as the first two of a long series of landings of saboteurs along the East Coast, it very nearly succeeded. Named for an early German settler in Pennsylvania, the operation was the brainchild of the Abwehr, the foreign and counterintelligence department of the German General Staff. It has been said that Hitler himself gave the order to begin sabotage operations within the United States, but his habit of issuing only verbal instructions makes it difficult to tie him personally to the plot.

The core of the plan was to use Germans who had previously lived in the United States and were intimately familiar with the language and American customs as saboteurs. While the idea may have appeared sound, it was there that the greatest weakness in the operation occurred. Selected to head the operation was Lieutenant Werner Kappe, a thirty-seven-year-old who had spent twelve years in the United States. The group he picked for the first two missions went through several weeks of intensive training in the use of explosives at an Abwehr training center near Brandenburg.

The men were shown photographs of specific targets and were provided with maps pinpointing the target locations. Among these were the Hell Gate Railroad Bridge over New York's East River; ALCOA aluminum manufacturing plants in Tennessee, Illinois, and New York; as well as numerous hydroelectric generating stations and key railroad sites through the middle Atlantic and Northeast.

On May 23, 1942, the eight men assigned to the first two missions were divided into two groups and given their assignments. The first group, lead by thirty-nine-year-old Georg Dasch, was put aboard a type VII U-boat, the U-202, commanded by Lieutenant Hans-Heinz Linder. Also put aboard the submarine was $50,000 in U.S. currency to be used for living expenses and bribes, and four waterproof cases containing a variety of explosives and detonators. The second group, led by thirty-two-year-old Edward J. Kerling, was placed aboard Joachim Deecke's U-584, also a type VII boat.

U-202 arrived off the coast of East Amagansett, Long Island, late on the evening of Friday, June 12, 1942. The four saboteurs and their crates were rowed to the beach in a rubber dinghy and put ashore, where they changed into American-made civilian clothes and proceeded to bury the crates as instructed. Their orders were to get themselves settled into nearby New York City and return at a later date to dig up the crates.

Having accomplished most of their task, they then had the misfortune of literally bumping into America's first line of coast defense, an unarmed Coast Guard beach patrolman. Despite the fact the United States was at war, men patrolled this long vulnerable section of beach night and day from a nearby Coast Guard station alone and unarmed. Seaman Second Class John Cullen quickly realized he had come upon something suspicious, but also realized he was outnumbered, so he went along with the story Dasch gave him that they were stranded fishermen and accepted a $300 bribe to keep his mouth shut and go away. He did go away, returning immediately to his station where he gave the first alarm about the landing. An armed group of Coast Guardsmen returned to the spot, but the Germans had already departed. The alarm was then sent up the Coast Guard chain of command to the navy department and the Federal Bureau of Investigation. The following day an army of investigators converged on the scene and dug up the four crates. It was now clear to everyone that the men Cullen had encountered were German saboteurs who had probably been landed from a U-boat. Meanwhile, the four Germans were on their way to New York City.

Arriving in Manhattan, Dasch and Ernest Burger checked into the Governor Clinton Hotel, while the second pair did the same at the Hotel Martinique. Dasch and Burger almost immediately began having second thoughts about what they had become involved in, and decided to turn themselves in. Dasch called the New York office of the FBI, but was treated as a crackpot and couldn't get anyone to listen to his story. Now desperate to get out from under the plot they were involved in, Dasch took a train to Washington while Burger kept an eye on the other two German agents.

At first no one at FBI headquarters appeared interested in hearing Dasch's story, but he finally did get an agent to listen once he explained where he had landed on Long Island.

Meanwhile, the U-584 landed Kerling's group at a beach near Ponte Verda, Florida. After burying their cases of explosives, the men took a bus to Jacksonville without arousing any suspicion from the Americans around them. Two men checked into the Seminole Hotel and two checked into the Mayflower Hotel. The next day one group headed to Chicago and the other to New York City, as Kappe had instructed them.

Dasch and Burger revealed the entire plan to federal agents, and eventually all eight saboteurs were arrested. Because of their cooperation, Dasch and Burger were given prison sentences that were commuted in 1948 by President Truman. The remaining six were executed for wartime espionage. For a while J. Edgar Hoover's public relations organization made it appear as if the Germans had been caught because of his bureau's diligence, but eventually the truth came out. We are left to wonder just how successful the two missions might have been, if Dasch had not persisted in finding someone in the American government bureaucracy who would listen to his story.

The failure of Operation Pastorius's two missions spelled the end of any serious concerted effort of sabotage in the United States by the Abwehr for at least two years.[25]

## Towing Missiles to America

The most potentially devastating weapon Germany had in her arsenal was the V-2 ballistic missile. It therefore stands to reason that some German officials had been thinking about a way to send at least a few of these missiles against American cities. Few of them would have expected such a limited attack to alter the ultimate outcome of the war, but as the war dragged on they continued to suffer from the frustration of German cities crumbling under the power of the American war machine while American cities remained immune to attack.

Born out of this frustration and the desperation to hit back at the United States was a top-secret project code-named Prufstand XII (Test Stand XII). The project is believed to have been the brainchild of Dr. Bodo Lafferentz. Head of the "Strength Through Joy" program that was part of the notorious Dr. Robert Ley's German Labor Front, Lafferentz also had a hand in developing what was originally called the "Strength Through Joy Car," later renamed the Volkswagen.

Lafferentz is said to have conceived of the idea and presented it to General Dornberger in the autumn of 1943. He suggested building a waterproof container in which an A4 missile could be stored for future use. He told Dornberger that "he had proved by actual experiment" that a single U-boat could tow three missile-bearing containers to a target area. Once in place, the missile would be fired at a target one hundred to two hundred miles away. Early the following year drawings were prepared based on Lafferentz's idea.[26]

While not everyone took the concept seriously, evidently enough officials did that a study was made to determine the feasibility of the task. The results were that the basic problem of getting the missile to within range of a target across the Atlantic Ocean was possible. In fact, it was found that a U-boat could tow three canisters with A4s inside them at the same time. The trip to either New York or Washington, D.C., was estimated to be accomplished in thirty days at an average speed of twelve knots. If the U-boat towed only one canister, the trip would be made in considerably less time. What appear not to have been addressed at this point were the odds of a U-boat succeeding in crossing the Atlantic while towing one, two, or three of these one-hundred-foot-long canisters. Remember that the missile itself was slightly over 46 feet long.[27]

Assuming a U-boat with three missile canisters in tow made it to a spot one hundred miles off the United States' East Coast, it was determined that three technicians could prepare and fire a missile in less than one half hour's time. This would reduce the U-boat's chances of being spotted and its vulnerability to attack to what many considered an acceptable level.[28]

Working at a control panel inside the sub, and connected to the canisters through umbilical lines, the technicians could open valves in the rear of each canister and flood the rear sections with seawater. Each canister, which made the trip towed in a horizontal position, would turn upright as the rear sections flooded to resemble what we now refer to as a missile silo.

Opening the hatch at the top of the canister, the technicians could climb down a ladder that gave them access to the missile's instrument section and its engine section for any required servicing. Once the missile was disconnected from the locking mechanisms used during transportation, it would rest on a gyro-stabilized platform in order to combat the motion of the open sea.

From a control room located below the missile, the technicians could fuel the weapon from specially made insulated tanks that kept the liquid oxygen and alcohol extremely cold during the trip. They could then make any last-minute adjustments, and finally, fire it. The missile's exhaust, which was composed of gases burning at 180 degrees, would be routed up ducts along the sides of the canister and out the top in the same manner as the exhaust of Soviet and American ICBMs that were fired from underground silos decades later.[29]

With the missiles gone, the technicians could flood the canisters and allow them to sink to the ocean bottom after returning to the U-boat for the trip home. In less than six minutes the missiles would slam into the ground and explode in or near the target area. As we learned earlier, the absence of a guidance system to control the flight beyond its maximum lift-off height left the missile's success at hitting a specific target up to chance.

Despite numerous and obvious technical difficulties with the concept, the tow-behind missile canister concept was assigned the code name Test Stand XII and given the green light in the late fall of 1944. That such a complex undertaking with such obviously limited chances of success so late in the war was even considered, much less acted on, demonstrates, in the words of National Air and Space Museum historian Michael J. Neufeld, that "desperation had come to overshadow all work in the Army rocket program."[30]

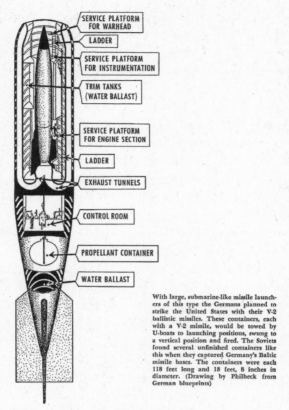

SERVICE PLATFORM
FOR WARHEAD

LADDER

SERVICE PLATFORM
FOR INSTRUMENTATION

TRIM TANKS
(WATER BALLAST)

SERVICE PLATFORM
FOR ENGINE SECTION

LADDER

EXHAUST TUNNELS

CONTROL ROOM

PROPELLANT CONTAINER

WATER BALLAST

With large, submarine-like missile launch-ers of this type the Germans planned to strike the United States with their V-2 ballistic missiles. These containers, each with a V-2 missile, would be towed by U-boats to launching positions, swung to a vertical position and fired. The Soviets found several unfinished containers like this when they captured Germany's Baltic missile bases. The containers were each 118 feet long and 18 feet, 8 inches in diameter. (Drawing by Philbeck from German blueprints)

German U-boat V-2 missile launcher planned for use against New York City. *USED WITH PERMIS-SION OF NORMAN POLMAR AND K. J. MOORE, COLD WAR SUBMARINES.*

Several important and talented engineers were assigned to the project. These included Klaus Riedel, Bernhard Tessmann, Hans Huter, and Georg von Tiesenhausen.[31] The Peenemunde engineers prepared preliminary drawings and a contract was awarded to the Vulkan Docks, a shipyard in Stettin, in early 1945. Vulkan agreed to complete the final drawings and build three test models of the canister. When the drawings were completed, actual work began on the three canisters, but Stettin fell to the Soviets in mid-April.

The fate of the three canisters is unknown, except that they did fall into Soviet hands when the shipyard was overrun. Reports on how complete they were are sketchy and inconclusive. Some say all three were as much as 65 percent complete; others, that one canister was completed and the other two were half complete when the yard was evacuated of Germans. Whatever condition of completion they were in, many believe the three canisters ended up in a shipment of scrap metal sent back to the Soviet Union, along with everything else that could be moved. Nevertheless, rumors persisted for a long time that the Soviets understood the purpose of the missile canisters, and brought them back intact for Soviet missile technicians to work on. The rumors might someday be proven correct, since we are discussing metal canisters that were approximately ninety-eight feet in length, and would have weighed in the area of five hundred tons each when complete. The truth is yet to be determined.

The accompanying drawings give the reader a rather complete idea of what the canisters would have looked like, and how a U-boat would have towed them.

The question remains unanswered: Could this project have succeeded? General Dornberger is quoted after the war as describing the tow-behind missile canisters as a "not unpromising project." Military writer Norman Polmar thought the "submarine-transported V-2s would have had a good chance of success even taking into account the fact that radar was then in use."[32]

Michael Neufeld thought the goal of the project was "ludicrous." He wrote that a few shots by sub-launched missiles would not have changed the outcome of the war, "but [would have made] Americans more determined to take revenge on German cities."[33]

In their history of the development of rocketry, Frederick Ordway and Mitchell Sharpe wrote that Test Stand XII "became a part of the history that might have been, given more time. . . ."[34]

Given more time. As with many of the other projects in this book, we are left to wonder just how close the Germans came to attacking an

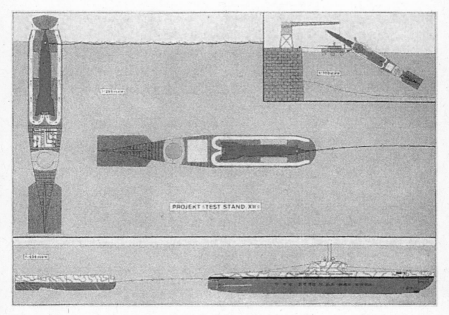

Loading and towing of U-boat V-2 missile launcher. *USED WITH PERMISSION OF JUSTO MIRANDA.*

American city. If they had started Test Stand XII a year earlier, they would no doubt have been able to build and test the canisters. The real challenge would have been in getting the U-boat, with its three canisters in tow, across the Atlantic Ocean undetected. Yes, with a little luck it might have reached a point one hundred miles off the coast, and with a little more luck might have successfully launched its missiles, but fortunately, we'll never know how much luck the mission might have had. Once launched, there was no defense against these missiles, and no way to stop them.

## FROM U-511 TO OPERATION TEARDROP

In at least one instance, interservice rivalry played a role in the German Navy's inability to strike at America. It was an idea based at least in part on one of the traditional tasks assigned to large surface vessels: shore bombardment. The key differences were that instead of a battleship launching large artillery shells at a land-based target, it would be a sub-merged submarine firing rockets at a land-based target.

The idea began to take form among the rocket and missile scientists and technicians working at Peenemunde. At the center of it was Dr. Ernst Steinhoff, head of the Guidance, Control, and Telemetry Laboratory. Steinhoff was thirty-one years old when he joined the Peenemunde group in July 1939. He was already famous as a glider pilot, holding the world record for distance flight in gliders, and had been awarded the honorary title of "Flight Captain" by the Luftwaffe. The following year he completed his doctoral dissertation on aviation instruments.[35]

Steinhoff's importance to the Peenemunde projects was clearly demonstrated on July 7, 1943, when he accompanied Wernher von Braun and General Dornberger on a command visit with Hitler himself at the Wolfsschanze to show him a film of the A4 in flight and to discuss the missile program. When SS chief Heinrich Himmler learned the three had flown to the meeting together, and Steinhoff had actually piloted the He 111 bomber transport himself, he "asked Hitler to forbid a repetition of this incident lest the leadership of the rocket program be wiped out in a single crash."[36]

In late spring of 1942, either Dornberger or von Braun requested the temporary use of a U-boat to conduct some experiments using army rockets. By coincidence, a type IXC boat was engaged in training exercises in the Baltic as part of the Fourth U-Flotilla and could be made available to the rocket scientists. The boat, U-511, was under the command of Dr. Steinhoff's elder brother, thirty-seven-year-old Lieutenant Commander Friedrich Steinhoff.

U-511 was a long-range U-boat that had been commissioned on December 8, 1941. Steinhoff had been her commander since then. The U-boat was tied up at a nearby dock, as technicians from Peenemunde went to work on her. They welded a series of six rocket-launching racks to her deck. The racks were from the Wehrmacht's arsenal and were normally affixed to a two-wheeled cart towed by a motorized vehicle, usually a truck in which additional rockets were stored.

The rockets, known as Wurfkorper Sprengstoff, were the third generation of rocket artillery used by the army. The first generation of solid fuel

German sailors preparing rocket launchers aboard the U-511. *USED WITH PERMISSION AND THANKS TO WWW.PRINZEUGEN.COM.*

rocket artillery was the Nebelwerfer, which translates to "smoke thrower." It was widely used, especially on the Eastern Front. The field piece, or rocket launcher, consisted of six tubular barrels mounted on a carriage similar to that used as a mount for an anti-tank gun. The thirty-six-inch-long rocket it fired weighed slightly over seventy-six pounds with a full charge of 5.4 pounds of TNT, and had a range of 4.2 miles with acceptable accuracy.

By the time of the development of the Wurfkorper Sprengstoff, the rocket had grown to almost four feet in length and 277 pounds. Its effective range was about three miles, and the open framework in which it was transported also acted as its launcher, so that the rocket troops were not required to unpack it from a shipping container and ram it into a firing tube. They simply had to pick up the entire frame with the rocket in it and place it in the firing position, connect the electrical igniter, and stand back and fire it.[37]

111

Wernher von Braun and Lt. Commander Friedrich Steinhoff standing near rocket launchers aboard the U-511. *USED WITH PERMISSION AND THANKS TO LAWRENCE PATERSON OF WWW.KREIGSMARINE.NET.*

As the submariners looked on, the men from Peenemunde completed welding the six-rack rocket launcher to the deck of the U-boat. The rockets had been made waterproof by the use of candle wax to seal their nozzles, and waterproof cables were run to a firing switch inside the U-boat. When the work was completed, "U-511 moved out to sea, heading for the small island of Griefswalder Oie, a half-dozen miles into the Baltic from Peenemunde. A short distance from the island, the U-boat submerged. The undersea craft leveled off with her deck about 25 feet below the surface and the rocket firing switch was flipped."[38]

The six rockets were launched at ten-second intervals, which was the usual routine for the artillery crews who fired them on land, in order to prevent the thrust of one rocket interfering with the movement of the rocket next to it. Each rocket burst through the surface, rose into the sky, and sped toward the target area. The tests were said to have continued for several days, until U-511 had successfully fired twenty-four rockets.

Dornberger reported that the men inside the submerged U-boat felt "nothing whatever" from the launchings. He described watching the scene from the surface as a "staggering sight," as he saw the rockets rise "with a rush and a roar, from the calm waters of the Baltic."[39]

These rockets were like artillery shells, meaning you aimed them in the direction of your target, fired them, and hoped they hit the target because once fired there was no way to control their direction. This made them virtually useless as a weapon a U-boat could use against a pursuing surface vessel. The chances of hitting the vessel were very slim. Without serious advances in rocket guidance, there was only one use for a sub-launched rocket to destroy large land targets such as ports or cities.

General Dornberger took the results of the tests to the Naval Weapons Department and urged them to use submarine-launched rockets against targets in the United States, including large cities, oil depots, and shipyards. "But the Navy refused to accept an Army designed weapon system." The following year the navy tested its own version of a submarine-launched rocket, but the tests failed and nothing further was done on the subject.[40]

But that wasn't quite the end of the story of U-511 and her rockets. Somehow, Allied intelligence had learned about the tests, and they would return to haunt Friedrich Steinhoff just as the war was coming to an end, and perhaps even cause his death.

Following the rocket tests, Steinhoff took his U-boat to sea for more traditional submarine duties. In August of that year, while operating in the Caribbean, U-511 sank two tankers, the Dutch-owned *Rotterdam* and the British-owned *San Fabian*, for a total of twenty-two thousand tons. The American-owned *Esso Aruba*, 8,800 tons, was damaged, but managed to limp into Guantanamo Bay.[41]

In December, Steinhoff fell ill and returned to Europe. He was then assigned to a staff position with the Seventh Flotilla. U-511 was assigned a new commanding officer, Lieutenant Commander Fritz Schneewind. On September 16, 1943, the U-511, her designation changed to *Marco Polo I*, was presented to the Japanese Navy by order of Hitler himself. The Japanese renamed her RO-500.

On April 1, 1945, Steinhoff returned to sea duty as skipper of the brand-new IXD2 U-boat cruiser U-873. She headed west to attack shipping along the American East Coast. The month before, the last U-boat wolf pack sailed from German-controlled Norway with similar orders. Because the Allies were able to decrypt the instructions being transmitted between U-boat command and the boats themselves, they knew who these boats were and where they were headed. It was Germany's "last major venture in the North Atlantic," and an attempt to "re-establish the campaign against North Atlantic convoys," and possibly take some pressure off the U-boats operating closer to British coastal waters.42

At the same time, tension was mounting in the United States over rumors that the Nazis were planning a last-ditch revenge rocket or missile attack on New York City or Washington. *The New York Times* quoted the commander-in-chief of the Atlantic Fleet, Vice Admiral Jonas H. Ingram, as saying such an attack was not only "possible but probable." The paper continued quoting the man responsible for the overall protection of the East Coast as he described how the Germans could get their "robot bombs" within range of either New York or Washington. "He might sneak a half dozen submarines off the coast. He might launch robots from the long-range planes we know he has. Or he might sneak a surface ship, disguised as a neutral, within range."43

Things went from bad to worse when Albert Speer, head of Germany's war production, announced over Berlin radio that missiles and rockets "would fall on New York by February 1, 1945."44

Hardly anyone believed this late in the war that German bombers could reach the East Coast, and although there had been reports that German technicians were attempting to build a missile that could fly across the ocean, few believed they were close to accomplishing it. The only way left to strike at American cities was a concerted attack with U-boats that had been outfitted to launch the "robot bombs" that had caused so much death and destruction in London. This was reinforced by persistent and reoccurring rumors that reconnaissance aircraft had taken photographs of U-boats in their Norwegian bases that had been outfitted with launching devices. In an effort to calm their nervous allies, the British admiralty sent a cable to Chief of U.S. Naval Operations Admiral Ernest J. King explaining, "There is no evidence from photographic reconnaissance to confirm preparations by the Germans to mount such attacks." It went on to claim that a V-2 (A4 missile) could not be launched from a submarine, but that a V-1 "Buzz Bomb" could. Unfortunately, it also made the claim that the damage from a single V-1 "would be so negligible as to make the putative project not worthwhile." It appeared they were saying there was no evidence the Germans planned a rocket attack against New York, but if they did launch such an attack, a handful of U-boats firing V-1s could not do all that much damage.[45]

Concern over an attack reached a peak when Enigma intercepts picked up a message from Admiral Godt to the U-boats he had sent out in March that they should separate from the group they had formed and work individually to "attack areas in American coastal zone."[46]

Suddenly all the reports and rumors about a U-boat attack against New York seemed to make sense. Here were the boats that were going to carry out the attack. The result was the creation of Operation Teardrop, which was a massive deployment of naval and air forces to stop six U-boats. At Teardrop's core were two hunter-killer groups consisting of four aircraft carriers and forty-two smaller escort warships. It was the "largest Allied hunter-killer groups operation in the Atlantic during World War II."[47]

Evidently the true believers in a rocket attack were reinforced when it was learned from Ultra intercepts that another U-boat was headed west in the Atlantic, commanded by Friedrich Steinhoff. Clay Blair says he's not sure "whether or not the Allies had made the connection between Steinhoff's U-511 and his U-873 and his work with rockets. If they had, it might have lent credence to the suspicion that U-boats intended to hit New York with V-1 missiles."[48]

Philip K. Lundeberg, naval historian and actual participant in Operation Teardrop, wrote: "The factual kernel of these emerging rumors," of a U-boat missile attack on New York "had been sown as early as June 1942, when scientists at the German Army experimental station at Peenemunde had carried out a series of test launchings of small artillery rockets from the submerged U-511 with the cooperation of its commander."[49]

To read about Operation Teardrop is to read about a naval force that appeared bent on revenge and death. An obviously damaged U-boat surfaces, and is surrounded by ships relentlessly shelling her back to the bottom before anyone on board could get out. The few survivors of one boat, U-546, were subjected to abuse during interrogations. The maltreatment of the U-boat's commanding officer, Lieutenant Commander Paul Just, prompted the captain of the U.S. destroyer that had pulled several of the Germans from the sea to officially protest the abuse. The interrogators wanted to know about the V-1 bombs, but the men aboard the U-boats couldn't give them the answers they wanted and suffered abuse for weeks after. They were treated as criminal prisoners instead of prisoners of war.

But the best was saved for Friedrich Steinhoff. After receiving word of Germany's surrender, U-873 surfaced and surrendered herself to the first Allied ship that came along, which happened to be the destroyer escort USS *Vance*. The *Vance* took the U-boat into Portsmouth on May 17. Steinhoff and his men were taken to the Charles Street Prison in Boston, where they were interrogated about the suspected V-1 attack on New York. Two days later, Steinhoff committed suicide while in custody.[50]

CHAPTER 7

# Target: New York City

WASHINGTON, D.C., MAY BE THE CAPITAL OF THE UNITED STATES, BUT New York has always been, and will always be, its leading city. To much of the world New York is America, and America is New York. The terrorists who attacked the United States on September 11, 2001, targeted government buildings in Washington with the apparent goal of disrupting the operation of the federal government, but their most visible targets were two New York City office buildings. The two 110-story towers of the World Trade Center were proof of the financial and cultural dominance of New York and America. They were the two most visible objects in any photograph or painting of the New York skyline. Although the terrorists might never have dreamed that smashing two airliners into the towers would bring them down and murder several thousand innocent people, they certainly expected to dramatically alter the appearance of that skyline.

## THE SYMBOLIC CITY

Before there were the Twin Towers, there was the Empire State Building. By the time the Second World War had begun, it was the symbolic representation of New York City, recognized by people throughout most of the world. It too was a target. The idea of aiming a bomb-laden plane at New York City's most visible building had occurred to several Nazi leaders. It had also occurred to some American government officials, as demonstrated by a U.S. propaganda poster that shows an airplane with a swastika clearly visible on it pointed directly toward the Empire State Building. Because New York

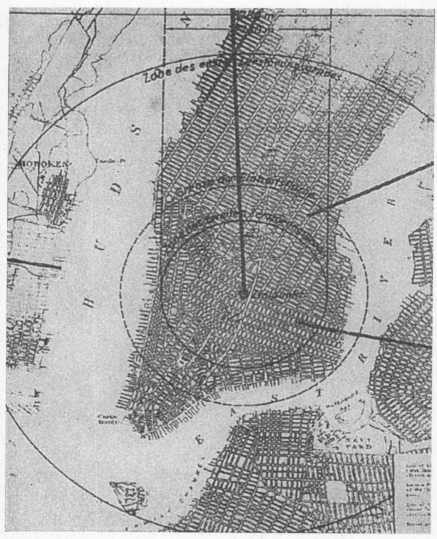

German map showing New York City as a central target for attack. *USED WITH PER-MISSION OF IGOR MOISEYEV OF WWW.COLLECTRUSSIA.COM.*

City was the world's best-known symbol of the United States, the Germans began as early as the 1890s to make it their particular target for attack. This continued throughout World War II, as demonstrated in some of the fanciful schemes that were suggested by various military leaders.

New York City, rather than Washington, was so often the target in the minds of so many Nazi officers, scientists, and engineers, that several of the weapons we have already examined in this book were sometimes referred to as the "New York Bomber," instead of the America Bomber, and the "New York Rocket" instead of the America Rocket. As the center of government, Washington might be assumed to have been the most likely place for a bombing raid that could damage our war effort, but more often than not it was the symbol of America they wanted to damage, New York City.

## THE PIGGYBACK BOMBER

This was an idea whose time would come, but not until a decade after the war had ended. It also demonstrated the high level of desperation on the part of Nazi military leaders for a way to strike a blow at the United States. Historian Thomas Powers described it as "the straining of military technology to catch up with military imagination."[1]

According to David Irving, developing a method for bombing New York City was discussed at several Luftwaffe conferences in May and June 1942. One suggestion that drew enough support to warrant further examination was the piggyback bomber. The idea was to mount a light bomber under the fuselage of a large long-distance aircraft. Both planes would be stripped of all unneeded items, such as armaments, to reduce their weight to the minimum possible. The larger plane would fly the full extent of its range toward New York and release the smaller aircraft. The assumption was that the smaller plane would be able to reach the city and drop its payload. There would be no question of being able to return to Europe, so the plane would be ditched at a specified location off the East Coast and the crew picked up by a waiting U-boat.

At first it appears that Field Marshal Erhard Milch vetoed the idea since the likely bomb capacity of the smaller plane would result in little damage for such a massive undertaking. On June 4 Milch, along with Albert Speer, who held the title Minister of Armaments and War Production, and a group of military officers and scientists, attended a meeting at Harnack Hause, which was the Berlin headquarters of the Kaiser Wilhelm Institute of Physics. They listened attentively to a lecture by Werner Heisenberg on atomic fission.

Throughout his lecture, Heisenberg never mentioned the word bomb, but Speer and company were there because the armaments minister had been told by General Friedrich Fromm that "our only chance of winning the war lay in developing a weapon with totally new effects." Fromm, who was both commander-in-chief of the reserve army and the army chief of armaments, then told Speer about a group of scientists who were "on the track of a weapon which could annihilate whole cities." So, Speer and Milch were at the lecture to learn about this wondrous new weapon.[2]

When Heisenberg's lecture was finished, Speer asked if this research could be used to build an atom bomb. Heisenberg responded that although it could be done, it might take as long as two years to accomplish. The Americans, the physicist told them, were much farther along in their research. Milch then asked how large such a bomb would have to be if it were to be capable of destroying a major city. He used London as an example. Heisenberg's reply was either that it would be the size of a pineapple or a small football. Either way, it would not be very large.[3]

Heisenberg told Speer he needed funds, rare materials, and the release of scientists who had been drafted into the army in order to further the research on atomic fission. Speer promised the money and the materials Heisenberg required, and indicated that Fromm would see to the release of the drafted scientists. He was true to his word. As for Field Marshal Milch, we are not quite sure what he had made of all this. It is possible that he was thinking about the fact that one needed only a single aircraft to drop one of these bombs on a city, as the United States would prove in 1945. We do know, however, that the issue of the piggyback bomber to New York was once again discussed at joint Luftwaffe/Kriegsmarine conferences. Discussions evidently went on for the next few weeks, but were finally dropped on August 21, 1942. According to the diary of chief of the air staff General Kreipe, the morning conference contained a briefing on the "long-range bomber operation against New York." Kreipe reports that the navy claimed it could not provide a U-boat to stand offshore the United States to pick up the aircrews. Perhaps in an attempt to change the navy's mind, he discussed the situation once more that evening with a ranking officer from the admiralty, and later again in a telephone conversation with the navy staff's chief operations officer. It was all to no avail, as the navy was not going to cooperate.[4]

Since the Germans were not big on suicide missions, which this would surely be without at least the chance a U-boat could rescue the crews, the idea appears to have ended there. This must have disappointed Milch, who knew Hitler was always ready to listen to outrageous schemes that required great daring.

## THE U-BOAT FUEL BRIDGE

Another proposal for an attack against New York City was born of German frustration and desperation. The idea originated with one of Germany's great aces of the war, Major Hans-Joachim "Hajo" Herrmann. The thirty-year-old Herrmann was a veteran of more than three hundred combat missions over England and the Mediterranean. He was highly regarded among the Luftwaffe leadership as the creator of inventive ideas when it came to aerial combat.

In 1943 he convinced Field Marshal Milch and head of the Luftwaffe, Reich Marshal Hermann Göring, that he could successfully combat nighttime Allied bombing raids using daylight fighters without the use of radar or ground control radio stations to locate the enemy bombers. Herrmann named his fighter group the Wild Boars. They used Focke-Wulf 190s, a highly successful aircraft used throughout the war as a daylight fighter and fighter-bomber. It was also used successfully for reconnaissance patrols. Instead of the usual tactic of attacking the bombers as they approached their target, the Wild Boars would hover high in the night sky above the target areas until the bombing began. Then they would locate the bombers by tracking their silhouettes against the fires in the city below or from the ground spotlights. It proved very dangerous since the fighters quickly became tangled among the bombers and the antiaircraft fire from the ground, but it also proved an extremely successful defense against the night bomber raids.[5]

Under pressure to launch an attack against New York as a payback for American bombing raids on German cities, Göring turned to Herrmann for ideas. The fighter ace was already prepared with a plan to use several of Germany's available long-range flying boat reconnaissance aircraft in combination with a small number of U-boats. The plan called for the flying boats to leave Europe heading west with their normal complement of fuel, but without their bomb load. At preset coordinates in the ocean they would land and be refueled by the waiting U-boats. Likely candidates for this duty were Admiral Donitz's Milch Cow tanker submarines, which would each carry the required amount of aviation fuel. The last fueling would take place some 200 miles off the Long Island coast. At that time the bombs that were stored in the final U-boats would be locked into the bomb racks of the seaplanes. The bombers would then attack New York and return to sea, where they would land near the surfaced U-boats. If inadequate air defenses appeared to make it possible to conduct additional bombing runs, the flying boats' bomb racks would be reloaded for a second and even third trip over the city. Eventually the aircrews were to sink their airplanes and board the waiting submarines for the return trip to Europe.[6]

The use of flying boats for such a transatlantic bombing mission must have proved interesting when Luftwaffe officials considered that Lufthansa airline had been making routine transatlantic passenger flights using flying boats that were refueled in the Azores for several years before the war began. In 1943 the Luftwaffe had at least two different flying boat models then in service that could have easily accomplished Major Herrmann's plan of flying the approximately 3,500 miles from Europe to New York. Two different companies manufactured them, each with extensive prewar and wartime experience in building successful flying boats: Dornier (Do) and Blohm und Voss (BV).

Originally developed for transatlantic mail service in the mid-1930s, the Do 18 was an extremely versatile and trustworthy aircraft. One version, the Do 18F, set a flight record in 1937, flying nonstop from Great Britain to Brazil, a distance of 5,214 miles, in forty-three hours. Used during the war primarily for long-range sea patrols and air-sea rescue missions, this two-engine flying boat had a rated maximum range of 2,715 miles. Her normal armament consisted of a machine gun and a .79-inch cannon. Without modifications she could carry two 110-pound bombs hung under her wing.[7]

A second flying boat capable of accomplishing the mission was the BV 138. The largest production version of this aircraft, the C-1, was powered by three Junkers engines and had a range of 3,107 miles at a maximum speed of 171 miles per hour flying at sea level, which is what Herrmann proposed. Armed with two .79-inch cannons and two machine guns, she could carry six 110-pound bombs.[8]

Of course, the deficiency of each these airplanes was the limitation on their bomb loads. Stripping away everything not required for the mission could have increased this, but even then the small bomb capacity would not be so great. On the other hand, the mission was contemplated not so much for its military value as for the psychological impact bombing New York City would have on the Americans and its effect on German civilian morale.

We do not know how officials of the German Navy reacted to Herrmann's plan, but it is likely that they responded in the same way they did to the piggyback bomber scheme, great reluctance to commit limited U-boat resources to what probably appeared to them as another harebrained Luftwaffe scheme. In the end, Hitler himself shelved the idea in the summer of 1944.[9]

## THE GREAT MYSTERY FLIGHT

We now come to one of the great unresolved mysteries of the Second World War, the alleged nonstop flight of a German long-range maritime reconnaissance aircraft from France to just off the East Coast of the United States and back in 1944.

Starting in 1942, several aircraft manufacturers took part in a competition created by the Luftwaffe for a long-range bomber capable of striking American targets, primarily New York. Junkers, the maker of several successful wartime aircraft including the Ju 87 "Stuka" dive-bomber and the Ju 88 level/dive-bomber, was an active participant in the competition. The Junkers designers decided to use their four-engine Ju 290, discussed in Chapter 4, as the foundation for an America Bomber. The Ju 290 was based on the original concept of a long-range bomber designed and built in response to General Walther Wever's 1934 request for the Uralbomber. Although only a limited number of the different versions of the Ju 290s were built, it proved to be a successful long-range maritime reconnaissance aircraft. In fact, three Ju 290s are reported to have made a successful round-trip flight to Manchuria to exchange documents and strategic material with Japanese forces, although some historians dispute this claim.

The Junkers designers made numerous important modifications to the Ju 290, including increasing the horsepower of the engines, extending the wingspan and fuselage length, and adding two more engines for a total of six. Designated the Ju 390, this new aircraft carried a crew of ten, had a maximum speed in excess of 300 miles per hour, and had a range of approximately 6,000 miles.

Two models of the transport version of this plane were actually built and flown. The third model was to be the bomber version with a payload of 3,968 pounds. It was never completed because in July 1944 a new order required that all aircraft production focus on fighters for the defense of the Fatherland. The Ju 390 proved to be such an impressive aircraft that Japanese representatives signed a licensing agreement with Junkers to produce their own version.[10]

One of the transports, Ju 390 V-2, was outfitted for maritime reconnaissance duty and assigned to the Kampfgeschwader 200, also referred to as KG 200. This was a special operations wing of the Luftwaffe that often engaged in long-range operations dropping Abwehr agents behind enemy lines. Because Germany had only a limited number of aircraft that could fly such long-range missions, this unit made extensive use of captured American Boeing B-17s and Douglas DC-3s, all with German markings. This unit already possessed at least five of the Ju 290s, so it was familiar with the basic aircraft.[11]

The flight whose existence historians are still debating is said to have taken place in 1944. It was a round-trip flight from near Mont-de-Marsan in France to a point approximately twelve miles from New York City and back. There has even been some unsupported speculation that British intelligence picked up word of the flight but hesitated to tell the

Americans for fear that U.S. air forces might be pulled out of England for homeland defense against German bombers.

One of the difficulties in determining the truth about this flight is that, as Austrian historian Dr. Marcus Hanke has pointed out, a great amount of Luftwaffe records were burned just prior to the war's conclusion. If the flight did actually take place, were the records of that flight among those destroyed? At this point, that question is unanswerable.

One historian who did quite a bit of research on this and other alleged German long-distance flights during the war is Dr. Kenneth Werrell. According to his research, the first public mention of this flight appeared in the November 11, 1955, issue of *RAF Flying Review*. Although the editors of the journal appeared skeptical of the claimed flight (this one said it was two Ju 390s that made the trip), the following March they published a letter from a reader who attempted to clarify the details, which included that one aircraft made the flight, and that it reached a point about twelve miles off the coast of North America just north of New York City.

According to Werrell, the story of this flight appears to have originated in two August 1944 British intelligence reports that are based in part on prisoner interrogations. The reports, titled *General Report on Aircraft Engines and Aircraft Equipment*, contain the claim that the Ju 390 took photos of the Long Island coast. These photos have never been found. The claim of the flight began appearing in an increasing number of books, but never with a reliable or researchable source given. Among the first books to mention this flight were William Green's highly respected *Warplanes of the Second World War* (1968), and *Warplanes of the Third Reich* (1970). Neither provides a source for the information. Several other authors then used Green's books as the source for their repeating of the claimed flight. Werrell reports that years later Green told him he no longer placed "much credence" in the reported flight.

After examining what details are available concerning the range of a Ju 390, Werrell concluded that although a round-trip from France to St. Johns, Newfoundland, via the shortest route (the great circle) was possible, adding another 2,380 miles for a round-trip from St. Johns to Long Island, made the trip "most unlikely."[12]

Adding to the mystery/legend of the Ju 390 as a truly long-range aircraft capable of reaching the United States was an article published in the *Daily Telegraph* of London in September 1969. The article bears the somewhat lurid title, "Lone Bomber Raid on New York Planned by Hitler." The piece quotes a former Junkers test pilot named Hans Pancherz who claimed the raid was to be carried out by a Ju 390 that "was built especially for this purpose." It continues with a claim by Pancherz that he flew one of the Ju 390 transports on a test flight from Germany to Cape Town and back in early 1944. Despite the success of that flight, Pancherz said the planned flight to New York was cancelled for lack of resources, and the plane he flew was burned to prevent it from falling into the hands of approaching American troops. Extensive research into this by the author proved fruitless.[13]

## Attack from the Azores

The Azores is an archipelago of nine islands located about 932 miles from and on an almost straight line out from Lisbon. They are a little less than one-third of the way between Europe and North America. They offered the possibility of an ideal location to land and refuel aircraft making the transatlantic flight in the years before such flights were a common occurrence.

Discovered by Portuguese explorers in 1427, the gardenlike volcanic islands remain a part of greater Portugal. The flourishing trade between Europe, America, and India in the sixteenth and seventeenth centuries made the islands a favored way station, with their sheltered anchorages offering safe harbor, especially in stormy seasons. Lufthansa, the German airline, used the Azores as a refueling stop for their prewar transatlantic flying boat passenger service.

The strategic importance of these islands makes its first appearance in significant German documents of the war on August 24, 1940. On that date Hitler approved the preparation of a draft plan presented him by navy Commander-in-Chief Admiral Erich Raeder. It was to be called Operation Felix.[14]

Felix was an idea on a grand scale. Among other things, it called for the capture of Gibraltar as a way to deny the Royal Navy access to the western Mediterranean. It also included the occupation of the Cape Verde and

Canary Islands, as well as the Azores. Raeder told Hitler that the capture of the Atlantic islands was a matter of urgency because he feared the United States might take it upon herself to land troops on the islands to prevent their occupation by German forces, especially if Spain and Portugal joined the Axis powers. The plan was based on the assumption that Franco's Spain would enter the war on the Axis side. Portugal might be expected to follow suit, but if she failed to, there was eventually a plan to send three German divisions across the Spanish border to occupy that country.[15]

Although Operation Felix never bore fruit, primarily due to Franco's reluctance to join the Axis powers, Hitler did not forget about the Azores. We have solid evidence of this in a memorandum written to an unidentified general by the Luftwaffe's liaison officer at army headquarters, Major Sigismund Freiherr von Falkenstein, dated October 29, 1940. Major Falkenstein describes his memo as a "brief resume on the military questions current here," "here" being Hitler's military headquarters. According to that document, "The Fuhrer is at present occupied with the question of the occupation of the Atlantic Islands with a view to the prosecution of a war against America at a later date. Deliberations on this subject are being embarked upon here." Falkenstein went on to describe the conditions "essential" for the occupation. These included Portuguese neutrality, and the support of both France and Spain. He summed up by saying the Luftwaffe needed to make "a brief assessment of the possibility of seizing and holding air bases (on the islands) and of the questions of supply. . . ."[16]

During this time at least two studies were undertaken concerning the Azores, as well as the other Atlantic islands. A naval officer, Captain Rolf Junge, completed one, while Major Falkenstein did the second. Both concerned the possibility of occupying and defending the Atlantic islands. Junge's study offered a naval perspective of the objective. He felt control of the Azores could be easily accomplished given the weakness of the Portuguese defenses there, and the ease of access to the islands from the French coast. The problem, he wrote, would be in supplying them and defending them against the Royal Navy, which continued to dominate the Atlantic. Falkenstein's study agreed that the islands could be occupied with relative ease through the use of pontoon-equipped transport aircraft, but he also foresaw that the lack of long-distance aircraft, especially bombers, would make defense extremely difficult. He suggested the use of flying boats for reconnaissance and combat missions around the islands, but also saw real defense as a serious problem.[17]

Two weeks later, on November 14, 1940, Hitler again expressed his desire to use the Azores as a place from which to launch attacks against the United States. With Field Marshal Wilhelm Keitel and General Alfred Jodl present, Admiral Raeder attempted to dissuade Hitler from continuing to keep open the possibility of a German occupation of the islands. Raeder's argument was that such an operation was "very risky" at best. He feared that violating Portuguese neutrality in such a way would give the British and possibly even the Americans a reason to land forces on the islands. Even if a German occupation of the islands was successful, he worried that it would push Brazil, still a part of Portugal, closer to the United States. The admiral had other plans for Brazil.

The Fuhrer would have no part of Raeder's caution. He "saw in the Azores the only possibility for carrying out aerial attacks from a land base against the United States in order to force it to build up a large anti-aircraft defense." His plan was to use the long-range bomber being developed by Messerschmitt, the Me 264, for bombing raids against American cities that would force the U.S. government to reduce its support of Britain's antiaircraft defenses in favor of its own. Raeder argued that the navy might be able to capture the main islands, but would have little chance of defending them against a concerted attack by the Royal Navy, and troops stationed there might face the possibility of not being able to be supplied on a regular basis. Hitler brushed this aside and ordered an "immediate inquiry" into the harbor facilities at the Azores for the landing of bombers and heavy equipment.[18]

Hitler's blind determination to attack the United States with land-based bombers is revealed in this incredible scheme to use an airplane that had not yet been built. The Me 264 was the only German bomber capable of making the round-trip flight from the Azores to the American East Coast, but it would be two more years before the first and only model ever completed would actually fly. Hitler had so deluded himself about the availability of this aircraft that he told Mussolini in early June that Germany would have a fleet of them ready to attack the United States by the end of 1941.[19]

Despite this reality, Hitler continued to cling to his idea of attacking New York and other East Coast cities from the Azores. On May 22, 1941, Raeder again attempted to get him to drop the scheme to occupy the islands. This time he made it clear the navy was just not strong enough to accomplish the task. Once again he was ignored. In his own notes of the day's meeting, he wrote, "The Fuhrer is still in favor of occupying the Azores in order to be able to operate long-range bombers from there against the U.S.A. The occasion for this may arise by autumn."[20]

What would be different about the autumn to make such a move possible? William L. Shirer believed it was because Hitler fully expected the war he planned against the Soviet Union would be basically won by then, and he could turn his attention more fully toward the United States. In fact, Shirer quotes Raeder's own notes that Hitler told him on July 25, 1941, in the midst of the offensive against the Soviet Union, "After the Eastern campaign, he reserves the right to take severe action against the U.S.A."[21]

Hitler wasn't the only national leader considering the Azores as a base from which to launch bombers against American cities. On May 24, 1941, President Roosevelt ordered preparations for the possible occupation of the islands by U.S. Marines. General Holland M. Smith, who later gained fame in the Pacific as "Howlin' Mad Smith," was placed in command of the Sixth Marines undergoing training for the operation.[22]

Hitler's attention was soon diverted eastward, never to return to the Azores again. He first had to send troops into the Balkans to rescue his Italian allies from their fiasco there, and then there was the pending invasion of the Soviet Union, which finally took place on June 22, 1941.

The few months he expected it to take for the conquest of Russia lasted several more years, until Soviet troops entered and captured Berlin itself. As for the marines who were training to occupy the gardenlike islands of the Azores, once it was determined that Hitler was no longer considering an invasion of the Azores, they were sent instead to relieve British forces occupying Iceland.[23]

# CHAPTER 8

# Dr. Sanger's Space Bomber

At the 1986 Farnborough Air Show, Germany unveiled a futuristic aircraft named the Sanger II. Projected to be flown in 2005, it was a two-stage low-orbit space shuttle-type vehicle capable of taking off and landing on a conventional length runway. The craft received its name at least in part because it made use of work done on ramjet engines and advanced rocket propulsion decades earlier by Dr. Eugen Albert Sanger. One small point the Germans who proudly displayed the plane did not emphasize was that Sanger's original design was for a space plane that was intended to bomb New York City. Of course, at the time, Germany and the United States were at war with each other.

## A Man before His Time

Born in Bohemia in 1905, Sanger spent most of his adult life enraptured by the thought of going into space. Like his contemporary and archrival, Wernher von Braun, he was a follower of space travel writer Hermann Oberth. It was Oberth's book *Rocket to the Planets,* published in 1923, which led both men to their life's work.

Oberth was a leading advocate of using a ballistic multistage missile for reaching beyond the earth's atmosphere. In his history of the development of manned space flight, Dr. David Baker notes that Sanger "never once contemplated space flight without a human participant." His idea was to meld the concept of a long slim missile to a winged craft that could carry men into space, and even to the moon. He anticipated that the first space flights would be made by a rocket-powered "stratospheric" airplane.[1]

In 1933 Sanger published a book titled *Raketenflugtechnik* (Rocket Flight Technique), in which he discussed the future development of an earth-orbiting space station. In the following years he authored several articles for the highly respected Austrian aviation journal *Flug* (Flight). In December 1934 *Flug* published a "special issue" that was entirely comprised of an article by Sanger titled *"Neuere Ergebnisse der Raketenflugtechnik."* The National Advisory Committee for Aeronautics published a translation of the article in 1942 titled "Recent Results of Rocket Flight Technique."[2]

Several more articles in *Flug* in 1935 and 1936 finally drew the attention of the Nazi war machine. In 1936 Sanger was hired by the Luftwaffe to join its research facilities, known as the Hermann Göring Institute. Although his primary interest had been and always was in rocket engine development, the Luftwaffe put him to work on the development of ramjet engines for fighter aircraft.[3]

The focus of Sanger's work was on developing an air-breathing engine that could serve as the primary power plant for a new interceptor. The French engineer Rene Lorin patented the original concept in 1905. Lorin's work proved that air compressed inside a tube, and rapidly expanded by combustion could provide thrust. By late 1941, Sanger was conducting experiments that demonstrated that by continually feeding air into the tube, and maintaining a steady source of combustion through a fuel injection system, the thrust could be sustained for a prolonged period. In one experiment, a sewer pipe was mounted atop an Opel truck. The truck was driven at a speed of fifty-five miles per hour, forcing air into the pipe. At the same time a steady stream of gasoline was injected into the pipe and ignited. The resulting combustion was maintained as long as the truck sustained its speed and the gasoline kept igniting. The next step was to find a way to control the exhaust so it would provide a steady source of thrust.[4]

The following year ramjet engines were successfully flight-tested. In each case the engine was mounted atop a standard aircraft, including a

Dornier 217E bomber. The engines worked marvelously, sustaining their thrust as long as the fuel lasted. One typical problem was that the engine mounted on top of the Dornier could theoretically reach a speed of 600 miles per hour, while the aircraft was constructed for a maximum speed of less than 350 miles per hour and a cruising speed of 248 miles per hour. Attempting to fly at the theoretical speed of the engine would likely have resulted in the aircraft coming apart in mid-flight.[5]

## THE SILVERBIRD BOMBER

While he worked on developing the ramjet engine, Sanger, along with his assistant and future wife, mathematician Irene Bredt, never lost sight of his original goal of building an aircraft that could reach into the upper atmosphere. As early as 1929 he had called this aircraft his *Silbervogel* (Silverbird).

According to Willy Ley, by early 1944 Sanger must have been considering the work being done by the rocket scientists on a winged long-range manned rocket, the A9 discussed in Chapter 5. Ley points out that the A9 would have to re-enter the denser layers of the earth's atmosphere at a shallow angle. Sanger considered the possibilities if the winged rocket's reentry of the earth's atmosphere was not through a shallow dive, but rather a steep dive. With wings designed for its mission, a rocket aircraft fired above the atmosphere would, in its descent, hit the dense layer of atmosphere twenty-five miles above the earth and ricochet off in the same manner a flat stone bounces off the surface of a lake. The rocket plane would be forced back up into the thinner atmosphere where it would continue its journey until it once again bounced off the denser atmosphere. This bouncing off the denser atmosphere would continue until the pilot altered the descent of his craft so it would reenter the earth's atmosphere as it approached its target. The result of these "undulations" would be to extend the range of the craft "to a surprising extent."[6]

As early as 1942 Sanger had added an additional name to his aircraft. Now it was also known as the *Raketenbomber* (Rocket Bomber). In this way it became an entry in the race to build an "America Bomber." Sanger estimated that his craft could carry an eight-ton payload halfway around the world. He attempted to obtain government financing for his project in a report he prepared titled *Ubereinen Raketenantrieb fur Fernbomber* (On a Rocket Propulsion Engine for Long-Distance Bombers). Perhaps because it appeared to be a project whose goal was too long term, and the war was beginning to turn against Germany so there was a need for quicker results, Sanger never received the funding he sought.[7]

In early 1944 Sanger returned to the subject of his version of an America Bomber. He and Bredt worked virtually around the clock producing a four-hundred-page report that was distributed in August to a small group. These included Wernher von Braun, Willy Messerschmitt, Werner Heisenberg, Professor Kurt Tank of the Focke-Wulf Aircraft Construction Company, Dr. Ernst Heinkel, head of the aircraft manufacturing company that bore his name, and Professor Dornier of Dornier Aircraft. The report detailed Sanger's plan for the bomber with the ability to reach the United States and to return to Europe.

His *Silverbird* was a one hundred-ton rocket bomber, of which ninety tons were fuel, which would be launched via a two-mile-long sled track. The sled was to be propelled by a rocket engine generating 610 tons of thrust for eleven seconds, sending the craft aloft to a level of about 5,500 feet. Once released from the sled and aloft, the Silverbird's power plant *would* ignite and the plane would climb steeply to an altitude of just over 130,000 feet, putting it slightly above the twenty-five-mile level of denser atmosphere. It would then dive into the thicker air, where its wings would ricochet it back into a long steep climb again. This bounce, along with most of the remaining fuel, would enable the plane to reach an altitude of approximately 162 to 175 miles above the earth. The plane was to continue in this manner until it was over its target. After dropping its payload, it would continue this flight pattern until it landed in Japanese-held territory in Asia. A simple retractable tricycle undercarriage would accomplish the landing. Landing speed was estimated to be about ninety miles per hour. Considering the craft's speed and the manner of its flight, accuracy of bombing a specific target was negligible. Although it was discovered that New York City had been identified as "Target No. 1," that bomb, had it been dropped, would have landed anywhere within a four-hundred-mile radius of the city.[8]

"Silverbird." Artist's rendering of the Sanger Space Bomber by Josha Hildwine.
*USED WITH PERMISSION AND THANKS TO DAN JOHNSON.*

What became known as the Sanger Report was translated into English in 1952 with the title "A Rocket Drive For Long Range Bombers." When the report was originally distributed in 1944, the German government considered the entire document a "State Secret." It was stamped with instructions that copying or photographing was forbidden, and that it was to be kept in a locked steel safe in a room that was guarded twenty-four hours a day.[9]

Following Germany's surrender, Sanger and Bredt went to work for the French Air Ministry, where there was a high level of interest in supersonic flight. They remained in France until 1954, when they returned to Germany. Sanger was put to work by the West German government developing a research center for aerospace propulsion. Over the years his Silverbird has had many nicknames, including America Bomber. It has also been known as the Orbital Bomber, the Antipodal Bomber, and the Atmosphere Skipper.

According to an account by Lieutenant Colonel Grigory A. Tokayeff, a Soviet rocket expert who defected to the West in 1948, a copy of the Sanger Report was translated into Russian at the behest of Soviet dictator Stalin. Writing in the *London Daily Express* of January 23, 1949, Tokayeff

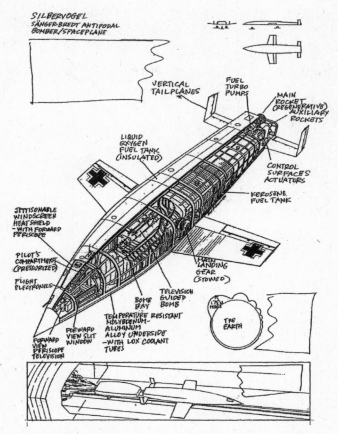

SILBERVOGEL
SÄNGER-BREDT ANTIPODAL
BOMBER/SPACEPLANE

VERTICAL
TAILPLANES

FUEL
TURBO
PUMPS

MAIN
ROCKET
(REGENERATIVE)
AUXILIARY
ROCKETS

LIQUID
OXYGEN
FUEL TANK
(INSULATED)

CONTROL
SURFACES
ACTUATORS

KEROSENE
FUEL TANK

JETTISONABLE
WINDSCREEN
HEAT SHIELD
-WITH FORWARD
PERISCOPE

PILOT'S
COMPARTMENT
(PRESSURIZED)

FLIGHT
ELECTRONICS

MAIN
LANDING
GEAR
(STOWED)

TELEVISION
GUIDED
BOMB

BOMB
BAY

TEMPERATURE RESISTANT
MOLYBDENUM-
ALUMINUM
ALLOY UNDERSIDE
-WITH LOX COOLANT
TUBES

FORWARD
VIEW SLIT
WINDOW

FORWARD
VIEW
PERISCOPE
TELEVISION

THE
EARTH

Detailed drawing of the interior of the Silverbird. *DRAWN BY AND USED WITH PERMISSION OF ELIOT R. BROWN.*

revealed to the world that Stalin called a meeting in April 1947 at which he had Tokayeff explain in detail the contents of the report. Also at the meeting were several Politburo members, the head of the Soviet Secret Police, and Stalin's son Vassili. Tokayeff claims that a discussion of the V-2 rockets was cut short by one of the Politburo members, named G. M. Malenkov, who said their range was too limited for Soviet purposes. He then exclaimed, "Do you think we are going to fight Poland?"

Photo of a scale model of the Silverbird. *USED WITH PERMISSION OF ELIOT R. BROWN OF KINGSTON VACUUM WORKS.*

Apparently the concept of a long-range rocket-propelled aircraft bearing the name America Bomber interested the Soviet dictator. Tokayeff wrote that he and Vassili and another Soviet rocket man named Colonel Serov were sent to Western Europe to search for Sanger and Bredt. Stalin's order to them was to bring both Germans to the Soviet Union in a "voluntary-compulsory manner." The mission failed, possibly because French intelligence agents learned of the plan to kidnap Sanger and Bredt, and were able to conceal their whereabouts from the Soviets.[10]

Although Sanger's Silverbird was never built, smaller wind tunnel models were developed and tested. In the 1950s rocket airplanes had a short but impressive lifespan, especially in the United States, where several were built and flown, but the development of safer and faster jet engines overcame the use of rocket engines as a means of powering aircraft.

# CHAPTER 9

# Invasion from the South

FOLLOWING THE FAILED 1898 CONFRONTATION WITH DEWEY'S FLEET in Manila, Germany shifted the locale of her continued rivalry with the United States to the Western Hemisphere. Two years later the Kaiser is reported to have informed his uncle, King Edward VII of Great Britain, that "German naval construction is directed not at England but America."[1]

Kaiser Wilhelm II is renowned among historians for the extensive and at times emotional notations he handwrote in the margins of communications addressed to him. This marginalia often revealed his inner thinking on a subject and what actions he planned on taking. His opinion of Germany's future role in Latin America was written on a copy of a telegram to Berlin from the German ambassador in Mexico City in January 1900, in which the ambassador voiced his opinion that a German colony in Latin America had greater value to Germany than did the entire continent of Africa. The Kaiser's response was to write: "Correct! That is why we must be the 'paramount power' there." In May of that year the German ambassador in Washington, Theodor von Holleben, cautioned Wilhelm that the U.S. government was deeply concerned about German plans in Latin America. The Kaiser's handwritten response to this warning was "Once we have a decent fleet this, to a certain degree, becomes immaterial. South America simply is no concern of the Yankees."[2]

At least a dozen times during the last decade of the nineteenth century and the first decade of the twentieth century, German warships took part in threatening actions in and around the Caribbean. There were

German plans to seize various Caribbean islands and use them as naval bases, and even talk of preventing the United States from building the Panama Canal because then the Americans could more easily move their fleets from one ocean to another if Germany and America were at war. The Monroe Doctrine, designed to protect the American republics from intervention by the European powers, was labeled a "species of arrogance peculiarly American" by German Chancellor Otto von Bismarck.[3]

During the First World War Germany attempted to win Mexican support for an invasion of the southwestern United States even before the United States had entered the war. In an infamous document known as the Zimmermann telegram, the German Foreign Minister, Dr. Alfred von Zimmermann, developed a plan to offer Mexico "generous financial support" to help her recapture lands lost to the Americans in the previous century, including Texas, New Mexico, and Arizona. The idea came to naught when President Wilson made its contents known to an outraged American public.[4]

## LOOKING FOR A SOFT UNDERBELLY

Unable to send either an underwater or surface war fleet large enough to launch a direct attack against the United States mainland, Nazi Germany sought another method of entry into the American heartland. Latin America, with its sprinkling of pro-fascist governments and anti-Yankee populations, appeared to offer an ideal opportunity. On December 2, 1940, William L. Shirer wrote from Berlin that "Most Germans talk more convincingly of a move across the south Atlantic." They expected that a German fleet, which included troop transports, could race across the south Atlantic from the French West African port of Dakar and reach South America before an American fleet could respond. They counted on the support of hundreds of thousands of Germans living in Latin America to act as a fifth column in support of a German landing. With a foothold in either or both Brazil or Argentina, the Germans could easily "paralyze any defense" these countries might attempt.[5]

On October 27, 1941, President Roosevelt revealed to a startled American public German plans for the conquest of Latin America and then the use of bases there to attack the United States. Speaking before a Navy Day banquet, Roosevelt informed his audience that he was in possession of a map drawn in Germany that showed how the nations of South America were to be reorganized under German control. He then told his shocked listeners, "This map makes clear the Nazi design, not only against South America but against the United States as well." British agents in South America had confiscated the map from a German courier. A former attaché at the German embassy in Argentina was said to have informed the British about the map's existence. A short time later the Gestapo killed him.[6]

While it is fair to say that a German invasion of South America was never high on any Nazi's list of priorities, the possibility that German agents were in Latin American countries working toward a long-range goal that might include such action cannot be overlooked. Several South American countries had substantial German, Italian, and Japanese communities that could serve as the basis for fifth column activities. By late 1940 it was estimated that Brazil alone was home to 830,000 first- and second-generation Germans. Argentina hosted 250,000, Chile 85,000, while tiny Uruguay and Paraguay had 10,000 and 18,000 respectively. Under German law many if not all of these people were considered full citizens of the Reich, and they were expected to remain loyal to Hitler's Germany regardless of where they resided.[7]

Perhaps the impact of these populations is witnessed in the reports from the United States naval attaché in Columbia, Captain John C. Munn, USMC, of thousands of Columbians pouring onto the streets of Bogotá cheering the news reports of German military victories in Europe during early 1940.[8]

In a chapter devoted to the activities of fifth columnists in his *Inside Latin America,* published in 1941, noted writer John Gunther reported that the German populations tended to live in their own close-knit enclaves, and were organized along Nazi Party lines under the leadership of officials from the nearest German embassy or consulate. Their children attended German schools and spoke German from early childhood. Such organizations as the Hitler Youth were very active, as was the dreaded Gestapo. Almost every capital city had a newspaper owned by Germans that spread the Fuhrer's message far and wide. Gunther described Latin America as the Germans' "easy route of entry to the United States."[9]

German agents in South America were working toward preparing the way for the future Nazi domination of the continent. In September 1940 eight German agents were charged with plotting the overthrow of the democratic government of Uruguay as part of a scheme to turn the country into a "German colony." The ringleader, the German press attaché in Montevideo, Julius Dalldorf, was quickly expelled.[10]

The fear of an outright German invasion to establish a base on the Atlantic coast of South America drew constant attention from Washington, long before the attack on Pearl Harbor brought the United States into the war.

## America Stands Firm

While all this German activity in Latin America was under way, the American government was watching with grave concern. As early as 1933 President Roosevelt, recognizing the potential danger in a continuation of the widespread anti-American attitude among many people in Latin America, instituted the Good Neighbor Policy. This effectively ended decades of the "gunboat diplomacy" that had protected American interests, usually commercial, in the region. U.S. Marines were withdrawn from countries over which they had virtual control. The United States agreed to help Latin American countries develop their agricultural resources, and sent experts to aid in education and health programs. It was a new Yankee image in the region.

Other, more direct steps were taken once the Nazi and fascist threat became a reality. By the end of the decade Roosevelt was lending support to American aviation companies to combat the powerful presence of German and Italian airlines that operated throughout South America. Pan American Airways and other U.S. carriers were encouraged to move into South America and try to muscle out the Germans and Italians.

An Italian airline, L.A.T.I., flew regularly scheduled flights from Berlin and Rome through Dakar in French West Africa and across the south Atlantic to Natal on the coast of Brazil. Despite difficulties in replacing planes and spare parts caused by the Royal Navy's sinking of German merchant ships heading to South America, by the summer of 1941, German-controlled airlines were still flying over three million miles throughout the Southern Hemisphere. Sensing that the Axis-owned or controlled airlines that formed a web over many of the South American nations were at the heart of the fifth column movements, the Roosevelt administration invested millions of dollars in helping Pan Am and others develop rival routes.[11]

The fall of France to the Nazi onslaught in June 1940 presented an increased danger to the entire Western Hemisphere. Throughout both Latin America and North America, the question of who would control the colonies of fallen European powers was being asked. The German conquest of Holland the month before drove the Royal Netherlands government into exile in Great Britain. There was immediate concern in Washington over the fate of two Dutch possessions, the oil refining islands of Aruba and Curacao. This was eased when the Dutch government in exile announced its determination to defend the Dutch West Indies and asked the United States for aid in doing so.

The French collapse presented an entirely different set of dangers. There were soon three different Frances. One was under the complete control of the Germans, who established themselves in Paris; the second was headquartered in Vichy and attempted to walk a thin line between the Axis and the Allies; the third was being formed in England as the Free French under General Charles de Gaulle. The question of which France would control places like French Guiana on the South American mainland, as well as the Caribbean islands of Martinique and Guadeloupe, was quickly addressed. Fearing the Germans would move quickly to claim these French colonies, the United States and her Latin American neighbors met at the Havana Conference of the American Republics. On June 30 the conference issued a resolution opposing the transfer of territories within the Americas from one European power to another. It also created a commission to administer any territory that was in jeopardy of such a transfer. Their obvious objective was to prevent the colonies of both Holland and France from falling into German hands.[12]

A special situation existed on the islands of Martinique and Guade-loupe. The former contained one of the best deep-water harbors in the area at Fort de France. Stationed there was a small Vichy French fleet comprised of the aircraft carrier *Bearn,* the cruiser *Emile Bertin,* the gun-boat *Barfleur,* and six new tankers. The training cruiser *Jeanne d'Arc* lay at anchor in the harbor at Guadeloupe. There were also 112 American-made warplanes at Martinique waiting to be transferred to Vichy France by the *Bearn.* An offer from Washington to use U.S. naval forces in the region to protect the islands was turned down by the Vichy French government. This raised concern that the Vichy French commander at Fort de France, Rear Admiral Robert, might either use his ships in support of the Ger-man Navy, or allow German U-boats to refuel and replenish at his ports.

Anxious to ensure the Vichy French fleet would remain at anchor, the U.S. chief of naval operations sent Rear Admiral John W. Greenslade to meet with Robert in August 1940. That meeting produced very little in the way of assurance that Robert would not be supporting the Ger-man war effort. A second visit by Greenslade, following a widely reported October conference between Hitler and Marshal Petain, head of the Vichy French government, at which it was feared the fate of the Marti-nique fleet was discussed, provided different results. Greenslade warned Robert that the U.S. Navy would sink any French warship that attempted to leave the harbor. He also demanded, and received, permission for U.S. naval ships and planes to enter Martinique territory for reconnaissance purposes. Robert remained true to his word. The French fleet remained at anchor until a Free French commander replaced him in July 1943.[13]

## RUBBER PLAN: THE INVASION OF BRAZIL

Brazil presented a special case for American officials concerned about possible Nazi and Fascist infiltration in Latin America. In many ways Brazil was the odd man out in the region. It is a Portuguese-speaking nation in a Spanish-speaking world. The only other Latin American nation that is not Spanish-speaking is Haiti. In the prewar years Brazil "tended to be more friendly to the United States than any other Latin American country." It had strong commercial ties with the United States and looked to the United States to help protect it from its more powerful oftentimes rival, Argentina.[14]

Brazil was ruled by what John Gunther called the "largely benevolent" dictatorship of Getulio Vargas. Both the nation and its ruler were strongly pro-American, but there were strong German influences at work for several years before the outbreak of war. One of the many things about Brazil that gave it enormous potential importance to both the Allied and Axis nations was its geographic location. Brazil juts out into the southern Atlantic Ocean, bringing the entire continent closer to Africa. Natal, a city on the eastern bulge of Brazil, is only 1,600 nautical miles from Dakar, in French West Africa, which was under the control of the Vichy French government, but 3,600 miles from New York. To quote Gunther again, it would be a "six or seven hours' flight for a fast modern bomber" from Dakar to Natal. Gunther spoke of a potential Dakar-Natal air bridge, especially if the Germans were given or took possession of Dakar from the Vichy French. He recommended that the United States seek Brazilian permission to establish a naval and air base there or at nearby Recife.[15]

Gunther wasn't the only American concerned about possible German troop infiltration of Brazil. Just six days after the Wehrmacht marched into Belgium and the Netherlands, President Roosevelt told the U.S. Congress, "Modern planes starting in the Cape Verde Islands [just off the west African coast] can be over Brazil in seven hours . . . and, Para, Brazil, near the mouth of the Amazon River, is but four hours to Caracas, Venezuela; and Venezuela is but two and one-half hours to Cuba and the Canal Zone." The president asked Congress for funds to modernize the American military so it would be able to defend the Western Hemisphere against a German invasion that would be a stepping-stone toward the Panama Canal or even an attack on the U.S. mainland.[16]

Concern over a possible German military assault against the Brazilian coast reached a peak on May 24, 1940, when British intelligence reported a rumor that a German merchant ship carrying six thousand troops was headed toward South America. The report also indicated other merchant vessels in the south Atlantic might also be acting as troop carriers.[17]

**THE ONLY "PAN-AMERICAN RAT HOLE."** *Bishop in the* St. Louis Star-Times, *1943*

1943 political cartoon depicting belief of Nazi agents in Latin America. *COURTESY OF ST. LOUIS STAR-TIMES.*

Although nothing more was heard about this German expedition, rumors concerning Nazi activities in South America, along with talk of a U.S. military response, continued unabated. They grew so incessant that on June 3, Army Chief of Staff General George C. Marshall felt compelled to issue a statement denying that recent American troop movements were the result of American soldiers being shipped to South America "to combat Nazi 'fifth column' activities."[18]

The German government also recognized the potential value of Brazil. It is reported that the Germans "sent more agents, recruited more local agents, and spent more money on intelligence gathering in Brazil" than they did in any other Latin American country. The Nazis attempted to send radio signals from secret Brazilian locales to U-boats operating in the south Atlantic informing them of ship departures, and their agents tried to sabotage Allied ships in Brazilian ports, but these efforts were successfully countered by American agents.[19]

Following the attack on Pearl Harbor and Hitler's declaration of war on the United States, the importance of Brazil to hemisphere defense increased dramatically. Fear of a combined fifth column and German troop attack on Brazilian airports at Natal, Recife, and Belem was heightened by reports that the Brazilian Army officers commanding troops guarding these airports were thought to be pro-Axis. The Brazilian Navy and Air Force were considered pro-Allies. As for Vargas, he maintained a balance between these opposing forces in order to hold on to power. Leaning too far to one side might easily produce a revolt from the other side.

Vargas walked the tightrope between his pro-Axis and pro-Allies military factions so well that American diplomats themselves were never sure what his true feelings were. Some believed he was pro-Axis, others that he was pro-American. A state department recommendation that he request the assistance of U.S. troops to bolster his defenses was politely turned down. Instead, Brazil requested weapons for its army to use in its own defense. U.S. military officials were reluctant to send arms for fear that they would be used against American forces should the day come that the United States had to take up the defense of the Brazilian bulge against a German threat.

American and British concern over the vulnerability of Brazil to an Axis attack reached the highest political levels when, on December 20, 1940, President Roosevelt and Prime Minister Winston Churchill expressed their agreement with a report submitted by the General Marshall and Chief of Naval Operations Admiral Harold R. Stark. The report concluded that Hitler's failure to achieve the rapid success he predicted against the Soviet Union might prompt him to turn his attentions westward and invade Spain, Portugal, and the French possessions in northwest Africa. This would bring the Luftwaffe within striking distance of the Brazilian coastal cities and their airports. The following day, approval was granted for a secret plan identified as the Joint Basic Plan for the Occupation of Northeastern Brazil. A group comprised of military planners

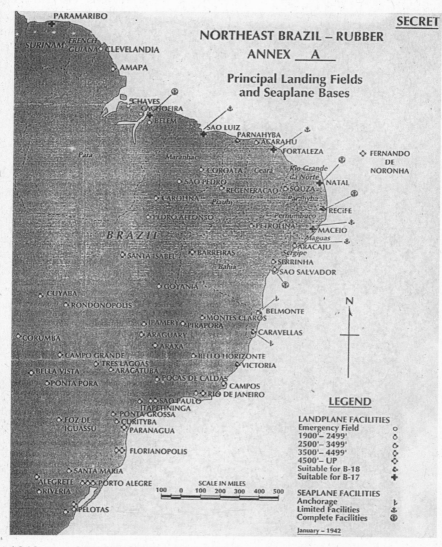

1942 map of Brazil showing potential landing locations for U.S. forces.

from the army, navy, and Marine Corps conducted work on this plan. It called for a brief naval bombardment of selected shore installations followed by a marine landing called Rubber Plan. Earmarked for the action were the First and Third Battalions of the Fifth Marines, supported by a fleet centered on the battleship USS *Texas*, the aircraft carrier USS *Ranger*, and twelve troop transports. Once the beachhead was secured by the marines, the Ninth Army Division Reinforced was to relieve the marines and become the occupying force, holding as many strategic locations as possible, with special attention to the airports. Should additional forces be required, the Forty-Fifth Army Infantry Division was to be in ready reserve. These forces, which were involved in amphibious landing exercises, were to be prepared to sail to Brazil on ten days' notice from the President.

In the meanwhile, the president's close friend and advisor, Undersecretary of State Sumner Welles, worked diligently to win the Brazilians over to the Allied cause before an invasion and occupation was deemed absolutely necessary. On January 28, 1942, he got the Brazilian government to break diplomatic ties with the Axis powers. Earlier he managed to obtain President Vargas's approval for the stationing of 150 marines at several airfields in Brazil under the guise of being aircraft mechanics. In May a Brazilian-American Defense Agreement in which American forces would help train Brazil's defense forces was signed, and the planned assault and occupation was dropped. On August 22, 1942, following the sinking of several Brazilian ships by U-boats, Brazil declared war on Germany and Italy. Two years later the Brazilian Expeditionary Force joined the Allied campaign in Italy.[20]

Although fifth column activities in Brazil attracted the concerned attention of Allied planners, the Germans were never in a position to attempt an actual landing at her airfields.

# CHAPTER 10

# Italy Targets New York

BENITO MUSSOLINI MAY HAVE BEEN THE JUNIOR PARTNER IN HIS PACT of Steel with Adolf Hitler, but Italy also had plans to bring the war to the United States. During the war the Italians developed several plans targeting New York City. Two were the product of the fertile minds of the special forces of the Italian navy; a third was an air force scheme that had more propaganda than actual military value. All were extremely ambitious in their concept, but with a little luck they might have succeeded.

## PIGS TO NEW YORK CITY

November and December 1941 proved devastating months for the Royal Navy. Churchill wrote, "our naval power in the Eastern Mediterranean was virtually destroyed by a series of disasters."[1]

This series of disasters began on November 13 when a German U-boat, U-81, commanded by Lieutenant Commander Fritz Guggenberger, lay in wait some thirty miles east of Gibraltar for approaching enemy ships. Italian reconnaissance aircraft had reported that British Force H was returning to Gibraltar after delivering forty aircraft to Malta. The war fleet, consisting of the largest British aircraft carrier in the Mediterranean, the *Ark Royal;* a second, older carrier, the Argus; the battleship *Malaya;* the cruiser *Hermione;* and seven destroyers, raced across what was known to be U-boat-infested waters at nineteen knots toward the relative safety of the Gibraltar anchorage. Lying directly in the path of the approaching ships, U-81 fired four bow torpedoes at 4:29 p.m., two each at the *Ark Royal* and the *Malaya*. Only one torpedo hit its target. It struck the *Ark Royal* amidships on the starboard side, flooding the boiler room. The screening destroyers drove the submarine down deep as they hunted her with over one hundred depth charges. Fire control parties succeeded in putting the fires out and righted the vessel by flooding portions of the port side. A destroyer came alongside and removed all crew members not working on damage control. A later investigation proved this to be a mistake. Two tugs arrived from Gibraltar during the night and took the carrier in tow. Within sight of Gibraltar a fire suddenly erupted in the carrier's engine spaces and proved beyond the ability of the crew left aboard her to fight. By 4:30 the following morning they conceded defeat and were taken off. Within two hours the mighty ship rolled over and sank out of sight. Amazingly, only one man was lost; the explosion of the torpedo had killed him in the first seconds.[2]

The second event in Churchill's "series of disasters" occurred in the eastern Mediterranean on the morning of November 25. While on patrol outside the British naval base at Alexandria, the U-331, commanded by twenty-eight-year-old Lieutenant Hans-Dietrich von Tiesenhausen, sighted a three-battleship fleet headed toward the port. Watching the huge warships through his periscope, von Tiesenhausen couldn't believe his luck at stumbling on such a prize. Although he could not identify them at the time, the battleships were the *Queen Elizabeth*, the *Valiant*, and the *Barham*. They steamed in the company of eight destroyers. The German submarine raced through the destroyer screen at high speed, maintaining a collision course with one of the battleships. At a distance of about 1,300 feet, von Tiesenhausen fired four torpedoes at his target and quickly dove to a depth of 820 feet, seeking safety from what he was sure to be massive retaliatory attack from the destroyers. Three of the U-boat's torpedoes struck the 31,100-ton *Barham*; at least one hit the ship's magazine. The battleship, ripped apart by the explosions, sank in three minutes. Over eight hundred men lost their lives. U-331 escaped without a scratch.[3]

The third week in December produced the final of this series of disasters, and one of the most spectacular operations conducted by the Italian navy. The loss of the *Barham* left the Royal Navy with only two modern battleships in the eastern Mediterranean. In contrast, the Italians had five in operation, two of which were relatively new. In order to safeguard these two vital assets, the *Queen Elizabeth* and the *Valiant* were locked away in the relative safety of the Alexandria anchorage. They were protected by every means at the British navy's disposal, including an underwater network of fencing that was opened only to allow friendly ships to enter or leave the anchorage. The Italian navy's assault teams especially concerned British authorities over a possible attack.

These teams made extensive and effective use of manned torpedoes, explosive motorboats, and miniature submarines throughout the war. They had been the brainchild of two brothers, Duke Amedeo of Aosta, who was general of aviation, and Duke Aimone of Spoleto, an admiral. Amedeo developed the idea of mounting small but fast motorboats filled with explosives between the floats of seaplanes. Prior to launching a bombing attack on an enemy anchorage, the motorboats were to be released in as large numbers as possible. While the enemy gunners were focused on the airplanes above them, the motorboats would speed among the enemy ships. The single crewman on each boat would aim his vessel at a selected target and jump overboard, hopefully escaping before the collision and resulting explosion.

Foremost among these teams was the Tenth Light Flotilla. From early 1941 up to the Italian armistice in September 1943, the Tenth was responsible for sinking or severely damaging thirty-one enemy ships for a total of 265,352 tons.[4]

The Tenth achieved its first "magnificent victory" in March 1941. During the night of March 25, two Italian destroyers, the *Crispi* and the *Sella,* steamed close to the entrance of Suda Bay in Crete. Inside the bay, in a highly protected anchorage, was the British heavy cruiser York, as well as the ships of a convoy that had brought British reinforcements and arms to Crete. At 11:30 that night the two destroyers lowered six motorboats into the water and turned away before the enemy sighted them. The motorboats, under the command of Lieutenant Luigi Faggioni, made their way across the bay to the entrance to the anchorage, a trip of about six miles. The shore on each side of them was under British control, and Faggioni's major concern was that enemy patrols would hear his boats.

Once they successfully negotiated the three net-based barriers used to deter enemy access to the anchorage, the motorboats rendezvoused alongside a darkened ship at anchor. They waited until the first rays of the sun brought enough light that they could more clearly make out their targets, and then struck. The result was a series of explosions in the anchorage that crippled the *York* so badly she never reentered the war. Three other ships went to the bottom of the bay, including the 8,324-ton tanker *Pericles*. All six Italian seamen were captured and spent the rest of the war in prison. The British admiralty was so embarrassed by the attack that for a long time the official records indicated the York had been put out of action by a German bomber raid.[5]

Nine months after the raid in Suda Bay, the Tenth Light Flotilla engaged in an even more stunning assault, the final event in Winston Churchill's "series of disasters." Following the sinking of the *Barham,* the battleships *Queen Elizabeth* and *Valiant* remained inactive inside the safety of Alexandria harbor through the middle of December. Just having these last two battleships in the Mediterranean, penned up for their own safety, was a major victory for the Axis navies, but no one expected the situation to last. Sooner or later the two mighty warships would venture back out into the sea and return to their combat roles. The Tenth Light Flotilla was ordered to prevent that from happening.

Italian naval reconnaissance planes maintained a careful watch on the Alexandria anchorage, photographing all ships entering and leaving or at anchor, as well as the network of obstacles and barriers that protected the anchored ships and the port from an enemy sea-borne attack. Meanwhile, a new secret weapon was being prepared by the men of the Tenth, manned torpedoes, or as the members of the underwater assault teams called them, "pigs." These "pigs" were approximately twenty-two feet long and twenty-one inches in diameter, roughly the same size as the typical torpedo of that time. Two men, clad in underwater rubber suits and breathing apparatus, sat astride the weapon with their feet in stirrups just as if they were riding a horse. The pilot, who was always an

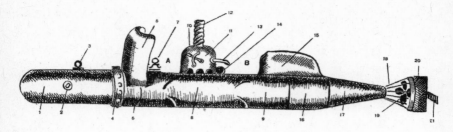

SLOW-SPEED TORPEDO—CALLED THE 'PIG'.

(*a*) Pilot's seat. (*b*) Diver's or second man's seat.

(1) Warhead (300 kg. of explosive). (2) Time-fuse. (3) Suspension-ring. (4) Clutch for warhead. (5) Wind-screen. (6) Fore trimming-tank. (7) Trimming-tank control pump. (8) Battery compartment. (9) Electric motor. (10) Crash submersion control lever. (11) Crash submersion tank. (12) Crash tank exhaust valve. (13) Security grip for second man. (14) 20 *atm* air container for tank crash exhaust. (15) Can containing reserve breathing set and working tools (net-lifters, net-cutters, rope, clamps, etc.). (16) Stern trimming tank. (17) Propeller shaft compartment. (18) Protective grid for propeller. (19) Propeller. (20) Vertical rudder (direction). (21) Horizontal rudder (for depth).

An Italian "pig" of the type planned for use against New York City. *FROM SEA DEV-ILS, JUNIO VALERIO BORGHESE.*

officer, sat in front behind a windscreen to protect him from the onrushing water while the torpedo was in motion. The man behind him served as his assistant.

The official Italian navy designation for the "pigs" was SLC, which was the abbreviation for "*siluro a lenta corsa*," meaning "slow running torpedo." Propelled by a storage battery, the manned torpedo had a maximum speed of 2.5 miles per hour, and an operational range of approximately ten miles. It could submerge to a depth of thirty meters. The two-man crew could raise or lower their weapon through the use of electric pumps that filled or emptied tanks within the torpedo.

On the evening of December 18, 1941, the Italian submarine *Scire,* under the command of Lieutenant Commander Junio Valerio Borghese, stealthily approached the Alexandria anchorage. Less than a mile from the entrance to the port the submarine released its load of three "pigs." Each torpedo carried a two-man crew astride it. The six men had volunteered for this mission without knowing their objective, but after being informed that their chances of returning safely were "extremely problematical." The lead torpedo carried the commander of the mission, Lieutenant Luigi

Durand de la Penne, along with Petty Officer Emilio Vianchi. Engineer Captain Antonio Marceglia and Petty Officer Spartaco Schergat manned the second torpedo, while the third carried Gunner Captain Vincenzo Martellotta and Petty Officer Mario Marino.

Their first goal was to find a way into the port, which was well protected by undersea barriers. Luck was with them, for as they watched from below the surface the underwater gates were opened to allow entry to three British destroyers. Demonstrating the courage and daring for which the "pig" drivers became famous, the three torpedoes slipped into the wake of the last destroyer, entered the enemy sanctuary, and headed for their individual targets. Each torpedo had a warhead stuffed with about 661 pounds of explosives and a timing device. Their instructions were to attach the warhead to a specific location on the hull of their target intended to do the maximum amount of damage, and attempt to get as far away as possible before the warhead exploded.

Despite some difficulties when his torpedo inexplicably stop running short of his target and dropped to the floor of the port, de la Penne managed to attach his warhead to the hull of the *Valiant*. Marceglia successfully attached his to the hull of the *Queen Elizabeth*. Martellotta and Marino were unable to locate their primary target, an unidentified British aircraft carrier that had earlier departed the anchorage, and moved to their secondary target, the fully loaded 7,554-ton fleet tanker *Sagona*. All six sailors were captured and imprisoned for the remainder of the war, but their mission was such a success that the loss of the two battleships was kept secret from the rest of the battle fleet for some time. Both battleships settled to the bottom of the shallow anchorage. The tanker exploded, causing severe damage to the destroyer Jervis, which was nearby. When informed of what had happened, Churchill described the actions by the six Italian torpedo men as "an unusual example of courage and ability." British Admiral Andrew Cunningham later wrote, "One cannot but admire the cold-blooded bravery and enterprise of these Italians."[6]

A year and a half later, a plan was developed to use that same "cold-blooded bravery and enterprise" against ships in the harbor at New York City. Born of the increasingly desperate situation of the Italian forces by

A Cant Z.511. This aircraft was to be used to fly manned torpedoes across the Atlantic and set them down close to New York City. *USED WITH PERMISSION OF GIOR-GIO APOSTOLO OF AEROFAN.*

early 1943, and the need to score a propaganda coup to lift morale, the Tenth Light Flotilla was once again selected for a highly dangerous, and this time somewhat dubious task. This time they would be delivered to their targets not by a submarine, but by Italian naval aircraft.

The plane to be used for this mission was the Cant Z.511, the largest hydroplane in the world at the time. Designed by Fillipo Zappata as a long-range transport capable of transatlantic flights, the Z.511 was to be used on the cross-ocean south Atlantic routes of Alitalia, flying from North Africa to Brazil. Work began on the four-engine aircraft in 1937. The first test flight took place in October 1940 and proved a great success. The original passenger version was theoretically capable of carrying sixteen passengers, along with its crew of six. It included a lower level for cargo and even had sleeping quarters for the passengers. With a range in excess of 2,700 miles, the Z.511 was able to land and moor in seven-foot seas. It was the aircraft's size, nearly ninety-four feet long, and ability to land and refuel in midocean that made it so attractive for the planned attack on New York.

The plan, which took form in the early summer of 1943, called for slight modifications to two Z.511s so that each could carry two of the manned torpedoes slung between its huge floats. The mission was to leave

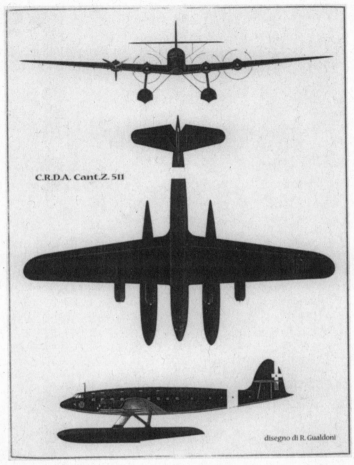

C.R.D.A. Cant. Z. 511

disegno di R. Gualdoni

Profiles of the Cant Z.511. *USED WITH PERMISSION OF GIORGIO APOS-TOLO OF AEROFAN.*

from Bordeaux, refuel in midocean from a German tanker U-boat, and alight off the southern coast of Long Island within range of the New York City harbor. The two aircraft were to approach American airspace just above the water, below any radar screens then operating as defense measures. Once successfully on the surface, the divers were to jump into

155

A Cant Z.511 being serviced. This aircraft was intended to deliver two manned torpedoes to New York City to attack ships in the harbor. *USED WITH PERMISSION OF GIORGIO APOSTOLO OF AEROFAN.*

A Cant Z.511 of the type to be used against ships in the New York harbor. *USED WITH PERMISSION AND THANKS TO ALBERTO ROSSELLI.*

the sea, release their torpedoes, and take them into the harbor to find and attack any available targets in much the same way the ships in Alexandria were attacked. The two airplanes were to return via the same route, once again refueling from the U-boat. No provision was made to recover the divers, who were expected to come ashore near New York and either seek refuge or surrender as prisoners of war.[7]

This ambitious raid never took place because the two Z.511s were damaged beyond repair during an Allied strafing attack. It was a daring plan whose success depended on a number of factors, including the arrival of the tanker U-boat at the right time and place, and the ability of the divers to find a way inside New York's protected harbor and locate worthwhile targets. Had they succeeded, the Italians would certainly have struck a propaganda blow against the United States and caused havoc in the harbor. One can only imagine the defensive measures that would have been rushed into place at other ports along the Atlantic seaboard.

## MIDGET SUBS UP THE HUDSON

New York City was the target of another daring plan that was to be carried out by the men of the Tenth Light Flotilla. This time the planned weapon was the midget submarine of the CA class. The Italians built twenty-six midget subs during the war of the CA and CB class. The C stands for *Costiero,* or coastal in Italian, while the A and B distinguished the series. The As carried a crew of two men and the Bs had a four-man crew.[8]

The CA was built by Caproni, and weighed between twelve and thirteen tons. In addition to her two crewmen, she carried two eighteen-inch torpedoes. According to Borghese, she was the idea of Lieutenant Commander Angelo Belloni, who anticipated the sub's use as a vehicle to get divers inside a harbor where they could mine enemy ships. The CAs actually saw little action, as the newer and less costly "pigs" served the same purpose.[9] The midget submarines, especially the CA, had limited practical use, especially since most enemy ports and anchorages were a long distance from Italian naval bases. Because of their limited range they could only function close in, hence their description as "coastal" craft. One method of solving this was to transport them to an enemy port on a larger vessel.

By the spring of 1942, Lieutenant Commander Borghese was in command of the Tenth. A plan was being set in motion to launch midget subs such as the CA and CB against North American naval bases and important ports, so Borghese had a CA sent to the Italian submarine base at Bordeaux to test her ability to force her way into a protected naval base. Arriving at the base himself, Borghese was given temporary command over the submarine cruiser Da Vinci.

The *Da Vinci* was one of Italy's largest oceangoing subs. She was armed with eight 21-inch torpedo tubes and two 4.1-inch deck guns. She had just returned from a solo cruise to the Cape Town area where her commander, Gianfranco Gazzana-Priaroggia, had earned himself a German Ritterkreuz for the sinking of six Allied ships, including the British troopship *Empress of Canada*.[10]

The deck of the *Da Vinci* was modified in such a way that a "bed" was hollowed out as a place to hold the midget submarine during the Atlantic crossing. Tests were then conducted to ensure that the smaller sub could safely be launched from the larger. The seaway between Bordeaux and La Palice served as the substitute for the American coast during these trials. Borghese reports that seeing one submarine mounted atop another was a "strange spectacle." After a check of her ability to navigate properly while submerged and surfaced, the *Da Vinci* was taken down below the surface and the smaller craft was released from the clamps that held her securely. The CA immediately rose to the surface. Her crew, waiting nearby in a rubber dinghy, boarded her, started her engine, and maneuvered around the area with no problem. Since the plan called for the larger submarine to wait off the American coast for the return of the CA, reattachment of the midget was also attempted. The tests were a complete success. Borghese reports that "The operation against New York had passed out of the planning stage into that of practical preparation." By this he meant the Italian engineers at Bordeaux could make similar modifications to other submarines in preparation for a multisub attack within New York's harbor.[11]

According to retired Commander Marc' Antonio Bragadin, author of the official history of the Italian navy in World War II, "Work was also begun to prepare an operation against the port of New York. . . ."[12]

mini-sub CA.3 - La Spezia, august 1943

Rendering of CA 3 minisubmarine to be used against New York City. *USED WITH PERMISSION OF RANIERI MELONI, SUB.NET_IT@LIA, WWW.SUBNETITALIA.IT.*

The Italians were anxious to send more than one midget sub against New York. Their problem was that at the time, they were short of submarines that could be modified for the task of carrying a CA across the Atlantic. They asked the Germans if they wanted to participate in the action by contributing a U-boat to the mission. German submarine force commander Admiral Donitz is said to have considered participating, but ultimately decided against it. He did, however, offer to provide the Italians with all the current information he had on New York City's coastal defenses.[13]

The operation received a setback when it lost the *Da Vinci*. On May 23, 1943, the submarine was entering the Bay of Biscay when she was spotted and attacked by two British warships. The destroyer *Active* and the frigate *Ness* dropped arrays of depth charges that caught their prey and sent the *Da Vinci* to the bottom with all hands.[14]

Although a disappointment, the loss of the *Da Vinci* did not prevent work on the intended attack against New York City from proceeding. As finally conceived, the plan called for several Italian submarines to deliver their cargo of midget subs to a position just outside the city's harbor, where they would be released. The two manned subs, each armed with two torpedoes and an assortment of limpet mines, were to travel underwater "up the Hudson into the very heart of the city." Under the command of Sub-Lieutenant Massano, the crews of the midget subs spent nearly a year preparing for their mission at the Lake of Iseo. Although the Italians realized that their planned attack would have little material impact on the

American war effort, they hoped that blowing up ships docked at New York's many piers would have an important psychological impact on the American people. By now, "The action against New York was in an advanced stage of preparation and had been fixed to take place in December."[15]

Preparations for the attack were halted in September 1943, three months short of the target date, when the Italian government that had replaced the deposed Mussolini announced to the shocked men of the Tenth Light Flotilla that it had signed an armistice with the Allied forces. New York was spared what would have been a shocking attack within her largest harbor by a group of determined and courageous underwater warriors.

## "Special Flights" to New York

As we have seen in earlier chapters, the Germans had some pretty implausible ideas for attacking the United States. Unfortunately for them, the Italians were not immune to the same level of thinking. While the Italian navy was working on plans to send midget submarines and manned torpedoes into New York City's harbor, the Italian air force sought a method to darken New York's skies with bombers.

In 1972, Italian aviation historian and author Giancarlo Garello wrote a two-part series for the journal *IARB*, in which he revealed these plans. The articles were titled "Obvietto: New York (Target: New York)." Keeping the same title, Garello updated the information in the articles with the results of his more current research for an article in the *IARB*'s successor journal, *Aerofan*. Another noted Italian historian, Alberto Rosselli, has substantiated much of what Garello wrote.

According to Garello, high-ranking officers of the Italian air force realized that the resources required for a transatlantic flight to bomb New York could not be justified by the limited strategic advantages to be achieved. Instead, they viewed such "special flights," as they called them, more of propaganda value at home, building morale in their own service and demonstrating to the Italian public that the air force was still a service capable of "great things."

Long-range flights appeared to have a certain fascination for the Italians, and they achieved some remarkable feats in this regard. In May

1942 a Savioa-Marchetti SM.75 made a twenty-eight hour round-trip flight from Rome to Asmara in the former Italian east African colony to drop propaganda leaflets. The following June a similar aircraft made a spectacular flight from Rome to Tokyo, stopping to refuel at an Italian-controlled air base inside Russia, and then again near Peking to obtain clearance to enter Japanese airspace.

The idea of a bombing mission to New York is said to have originated in the spring of 1942 with Nicolo Lana, chief test pilot of aircraft manufacturer Piaggio. He approached the Air Ministry with the proposal to use the three-engine long-range P.23R for his New York raid. The P.23R had already set several prewar records for speed and distance, but was not being used for wartime duties. Lana proposed to arm the P.23R with a single 2,200-pound bomb to be dropped on the center of the city. The aircraft would be overfilled with fuel to help extend its range. He proposed to fly the plane himself, along with a single flight engineer named Maiao. Balancing the weight of the additional fuel following an overloaded take-off, Lana proposed to cruise on all three engines, using the minimum fuel consumption settings. As the weight of the fuel declined, he would cut one engine, then later a second, making the last part of the trip on a single engine. After dropping his bomb on New York, Lana proposed to ditch the plane, which now would not have enough fuel to return to Europe, near the Nantucket Lighthouse, where an Italian submarine would be waiting for him and his flight engineer.

Evidently the air force, which considered Lana a mere civilian despite his membership in the air force reserve, rejected his plan. They might have considered trying the flight with a regular air force pilot, but the P.23R Lana proposed to use, the only one in existence, was severely damaged while trying to land in a strong crosswind at a small airfield near Albenga.

Meanwhile, the Air Staff was considering using the Z.511A for a bombing raid on New York. This was the air force's version of the same aircraft the navy was planning to use to deliver the manned torpedoes into New York's harbor. The Chief of the Air Staff, General Rino Corso Fougier, ordered a study on the technical feasibility of the huge floatplane successfully making the transatlantic flight. Because such a long flight

The Piaggio P.23R that was intended for a single bombing raid on New York City. It was destroyed in an accident before it could be used. *USED WITH PERMISSION OF GIORGIO APOSTOLO OF AEROFAN.*

would limit the bomb payload of the Z.511A, someone had what Alberto Rosselli called the "odd idea" of dropping one small bomb on New York; the aircraft should also drop one ton of Italian propaganda leaflets printed with the tricolors of Italy.

At a February 7, 1943, meeting at air force headquarters, it was decided that a midocean refueling was not realistic considering the need for maintaining radio silence to prevent enemy ships from attacking the submarine and aircraft while the fueling was in progress. The men present recognized something the navy had evidently overlooked; without radio contact, the chance of the tanker submarine and the airplane arriving at the correct location at the same time was slight. The plane and its crew might end up being tossed around the surface of the ocean for days and eventually lost without enough fuel to return to Bordeaux. As a result, the Z.511A was scratched from the air force's plans.

Instead of a floatplane, it was decided to attempt the flight with the latest land-based airplane from Savoia-Marchetti, the company that built the plane that had earlier flown from Rome to Tokyo. At the time the SM.95 was being prepared for its first full test flight. Seventy-three feet long, with a 112-foot wingspan, the four-engine SM.95 saw service after the war as an Alitalia airliner carrying twenty-four passengers. With

Savoia-Marchetti SM.95 planned for a bombing mission against New York City.
*USED WITH PERMISSION AND THANKS TO ALBERTO ROSSELLI.*

modifications recommended by an air force committee, she was expected to have a nonstop range of between 6,835 and 7,456 miles, allowing for the weight of two 550-pound bombs. The bombs weren't going to cause much damage to New York, but again the Italians considered that the success of such a flight would have great morale and propaganda value.

The aircraft destined for this mission was prepared for its first military test flights on September 2, 1943. Six days later the Italian government announced the surprising news that it had signed an armistice with the Allies, and the project was halted.[16]

# CHAPTER 11

# Why They Failed

WE BEGAN WITH THE QUESTION: "HOW CLOSE DID NAZI GERMANY come to launching a meaningful attack on the United States?" If we define "meaningful attack" as one that would have had a significant impact on the American war effort, then the answer is that they did not even come close. But, if we define "meaningful attack" as one that would have had an impact on the morale of the American people, or perhaps one that demonstrated that our nation was not immune to assault by an enemy power, then perhaps they came a lot closer than we had previously believed. Fascist Italy came close to accomplishing such an attack as well.

A lone bomber on a one-way mission, dropping even a small number of bombs on New York City, or perhaps the Capitol building or the White House, would have shaken the American public's confidence in our armed forces' ability to protect our own borders. The same effect would have resulted had Italian midget submarines or the so-called "pigs" blown up a few ships at New York's docks, or if U-boats had managed to get close enough to our shore, again, to fire a few missiles into population centers.

Attacks of this nature would not have altered the outcome of the war. If anything, they would have made the American people more united in their determination to defeat the European fascists, in much the same way the attack on Pearl Harbor resulted in a determination to bring the Japanese Empire to its knees. In the same way the Japanese "sneak attack" resulted in the cry, "Remember Pearl Harbor," a successful German attack, even one of little noteworthy impact, would have inspired a similar war cry with its accompanied desire for revenge; a retaliation that could only have cost more German lives and more destruction of German cities.

In the end, as we know, Germany never succeeded in actually attacking the U.S. mainland. It was not, as we have seen in the preceding chapters, for want of trying. The desire was there, but the ability lagged behind. There were several basic reasons for this failure.

## The Incomplete Air Force

Germany began the war with a significant lead in air technology, but the Luftwaffe never became a force with a strategic vision. Such a vision would have provided the impetus to produce aircraft capable of reaching the United States early in the war. When General Wever died in 1936, the dream of building a strategic air force all but died with him.

The Luftwaffe fought to the end with air fleets mostly comprised of aircraft models utilized in its first strikes against Poland. The development of heavy bombers capable of carrying large payloads long distances never materialized. Göring complained that they were too expensive when compared to a medium-range bomber. Then there was the constant requirement that bombers be able to perform as dive-bombers as well as level bombers. The effect was that the Luftwaffe never expanded beyond its original mission of supporting ground troops.[1]

The long-term failure of this role became obvious following the German invasion of the Soviet Union. Although the initial attacks inflicted tremendous damage on the Soviet air force in terms of aircraft lost and damaged, the Soviets were able to replace the lost planes rapidly because their important aircraft production plants were located near or beyond the Ural Mountains, out of range of German bombers. The situation might have been different if Wever's Uralbomber had been put into serial production.[2]

The Germans believed in the lightning war, the *blitzkrieg*. In this philosophy there was no need for long-range heavy bombers to strike targets deep within an enemy country. Dive-bombers and medium-level bombers could destroy enemy installations close to the front and weaken resistance to the army's advance, as they did so successfully during the first half of the war. But, when the war moved beyond the front, in the way it did for the Allies as they bombed so much German production capacity into rubble before the first Allied soldier landed in Western Europe, Germany had no means of retaliating with any critical result. The Luftwaffe was never a complete air force intended to fight a world war. By the time the Germans realized their own shortcoming, it was too late to catch up. When the war began, the Luftwaffe was the largest air force in the world, with in excess of 4,000 frontline aircraft. Behind that impressive number was an organizational structure appropriate for homeland defense, but ill-suited for the task of carrying the battle far beyond the German frontier. It never truly succeeded in doing this.[3]

By contrast, the United States Army Air Forces began the war with less than two thousand aircraft. Perhaps because we felt relatively safe from enemy attack, the air force we built was intended as an aggressive force meant to bring the fight to the enemy, not for defense. By March 1945, 7,177 American bombers were engaged in flying combat missions over Europe alone. This does not include thousands more operating in the Pacific.[4]

The Germans may have dreamed of building aircraft that could fly across the Atlantic Ocean and bomb American cities in revenge for the American bombers that darkened the daytime skies of German cities, but they would not succeed in sending even one bomber to New York or Washington because they had lacked the vision to develop an air force capable of such a strategic mission. They had failed to build a complete air force.

## Squandered Resources

If Germany was to attack the United States with long-range bombers or intercontinental missiles, it was not going to do it with the methods used for research and development. Nazi Germany lacked a central authority with responsibility for the development and construction of advanced weaponry, similar to the Manhattan Project that built the world's first two atom bombs. Without such an authority, German scientists and engineers had to compete with each other for resources that grew increasingly scarce as the war dragged on. Rivalry between the military establishment and industry leaders for funding resulted in many more projects begun than could ever be completed. Added to this was the constant inter-ference by Nazi officials who often knew little of the military value of the projects, but were driven by a need to bring them under their own control to increase their power in the political system.

Hitler himself is at fault for much of the failure to develop advanced weaponry. He engaged in an on-and-off relationship with the need to invest in long-term development. Often his attention would be drawn to some new project that he was told could produce the "miracle weapons" he sought, and money and resources would be diverted from weapons devel-opment projects that offered more substantial results, and were less sensa-tional. Projects that should have been funded early on, such as the America Bomber, often languished on the sidelines while others that held little hope of success received enough funds and materials to keep them alive.

In the end, Germany did not run out of ideas for ways to attack the United States, it simply ran out of resources, manpower, and time.

# Notes

*Introduction*

1. Patrick J. Buchanan, *A Republic, Not an Empire* (Washington, D.C.: Regnery & Co., 1999), 278.
2. "Robot Bomb Attack Feared," *The New York Times,* January 21, 1945.
3. Lt. A. Carter, "It Can Be Done," *Canadian Defence Quarterly* 16 (October 1938): 54.


*Chapter 1: Before There Was a Hitler*

1. Bundesarchiv-Militararchiv (Federal Military Archive), Freiburg, Germany, F 5174b, vol. I, 163–67, as quoted in Holger H. Herwig, *Politics of Frustration: The United States in German Naval Planning, 1889–1941* (Boston: Little, Brown & Co., 1976), 86.
2. Bundesarchiv-Militararchiv (Federal Military Archive), Freiburg, Germany, F 3677, vol. I, as quoted in Herwig, *Politics of Frustration,* 43.
3. H. Paul Jeffers, *Colonel Roosevelt: Theodore Roosevelt Goes to War 1897–1898* (New York: John Wiley & Sons, 1996), 40.
4. Bundesarchiv-Militararchiv (Federal Military Archive), Freiburg, Germany, F 5174b, vol. I, 68–92, as cited in Herwig, *Politics of Frustration,* 43–47.
5. Michael Gannon, *Operation Drumbeat* (New York: Harper & Row Publishers, 1990), 69.
6. Herwig, *Politics of Frustration,* 45.
7. Ibid., 48.
8. Ibid., 52–59.
9. Ibid., 85–86.
10. G. J. A. O'Toole, *The Spanish War: An American Epic—1898* (New York: W. W. Norton, 1984), 191–192, 251.
11. Herwig, *Politics of Frustration,* 32–33.
12. Ibid., 31–32.
13. Nathan Sargent, USN, *Admiral Dewey and the Manila Campaign* (Washington, D.C.: Naval Historical Foundation, 1947), 79–87.
14. Michael Dorman, *The Secret Service Story* (New York: Delacorte Press, 1967), 128–132.
15. Lee Kennett, *A History of Strategic Bombing* (New York: Scribner's Sons, 1982), 37–38.


*Chapter 2: Adolf Hitler, America, and the World*

1. Hugh R. Trevor-Roper, ed., *Hitler's Table Talk, 1941–1944* (London: Weidenfeld & Nicolson, 1953), 188.
2. Gerhard L. Weinberg, *World in the Balance: Behind the Scenes of World War II* (Hanover, NH: University Press of New England, 1981), 53.
3. Norman J. W. Goda, *Tomorrow the World: Hitler, Northwest Africa, and the Path toward America* (College Station: Texas A&M University Press, 1998), xviii; Gerhard L. Weinberg, ed., *Hitlers Zweites Buch: Ein Dokument aus dem Jahr 1928.* (Stuttgart: Deutsche Verlags-Anstalt, 1961), 131–132.

4. Alan Bullock, *Hitler: A Study in Tyranny* (New York: Konecky & Konecky, 1999), 57.

5. Martin Gilbert, *The First World War: A Complete History* (New York: Henry Holt and Co., 1994) 499.

6. Ibid., 503.

7. H. Paul Jeffers, *Colonel Roosevelt: Theodore Roosevelt Goes to War 1897–1898* (New York: John Wiley & Sons, 1996), 139. The article appeared in the newspaper Heraldo.

8. Richard Grunberger, *The 12-Year Reich: A Social History of Nazi Germany 1933–1945* (New York: Holt, Rinehart and Winston, 1971), 33.

9. Bullock, *Hitler,* 662.

10. Ibid., 121; William L. Shirer, *The Rise and Fall of the Third Reich: A History of Nazi Germany* (New York: Simon and Schuster, 1960), 80–81.

11. Gerhard L. Weinberg, *Germany, Hitler, and World War II* (New York: Cambridge University Press, 1996), 50.

12. Ibid., 50.

13. Trevor-Roper, *Hitler's Table Talk,* 188.

14. Grunberger, *The 12-Year Reich,* 33.

15. Holger H. Herwig, *Politics of Frustration* (Englewood Cliffs, NJ: Prentice-Hall, 1979), 184.

16. David Kahn, *Hitler's Spies: German Military Intelligence in World War II* (New York: Macmillan Publishing Co., 1978), 80–84.

17. Shirer, *Rise and Fall,* 749f.

18. "Military information page No. 14: Special features of American combat procedures since the beginning of the German counter attack to December 16, 1944," National Archives, RG 242, T78, Roll 442, Frame 6415736.

19. Weinberg, *Germany,* 28.

20. Thomas A. Bailey and Paul Bryan, *Hitler vs. Roosevelt: The Undeclared Naval War* (New York: The Free Press, 1979), 269.

21. Weinberg, *World in the Balance,* 80–90.

22. Bullock, *Hitler,* 663.

23. James V. Compton, *The Swastika and the Eagle* (Boston: Houghton Mifflin Co., 1967), 259.

24. Gerhard L. Weinberg, e-mail to the author dated August 25, 2001.

### Chapter 3: The Plan to Bomb America

1. Holger H. Herwig, *Politics of Frustration: The United States in German Naval Planning, 1889–1941* (Boston: Little, Brown & Co., 1976), 215, 223, 241.

2. Ibid., 241.

3. John Peet, "Berlin Notebook," *German Democratic Report,* October 4, 1972.

4. David Kahn, *Hitler's Spies: German Military Intelligence in World War II* (New York: Macmillan Publishing Co., 1978), 157.

5. Ibid.

6. Nicolaus von Below, *At Hitler's Side* (London: Greenhill Books, 2001), 92.

7. David Irving, *The Rise and Fall of the Luftwaffe: The Life of Field Marshal Erhard Milch* (Boston: Little, Brown & Co., 1973), 153.

8. Louis L. Snyder, *Louis L. Snyder's Historical Guide to World War II* (Westport, CT: Greenwood Press, 1982), 265.

9. Irving, *Rise and Fall,* 164.

10. Ibid., 211.

11. Kahn, *Hitler's Spies,* 386.

12. Ibid., 158–159.

13. Dietrich H. Schwenke, interview by David Kahn, September 18, 1973.

14. Translation by Gerry Trampler.

15. Translation by John Peet, *Democratic German Report,* October 4, 1972.

16. Translation by Robert L. Waddell.

## *Chapter 4: The Race to Build the America Bomber*

1. Prosecution Document R-140, Exhibit USA-160, International Military Tribunal, December 10, 1945, 388–89. The full text can be found at The Mazal Library, online at www.mazal.org.

2. David Irving, *The Rise and Fall of the Luftwaffe: The Life of Field Marshal Erhard Milch* (Boston: Little, Brown & Co., 1973), 245.

3. Ibid.

4. *The New York Times,* May 29, 1942, p. 1.

5. Forrest C. Pogue, *George C. Marshall,* 3 vols. (New York: Viking Press, 1963–1973), 2: 18.

6. Robert Dallek, *Franklin D. Roosevelt and American Foreign Policy, 1939–1945* (New York: Oxford University Press, 1979), 221–222.

7. Fred Allhoff, *Lightning in the Night* (Englewood Cliffs, NJ: Prentice-Hall, Inc., 1979).

8. George W. Smith, *Carlson's Raid* (Novato, CA: Presidio Press, 2001), 1.

9. Kenneth Schaffel, *The Emerging Shield* (Washington, D.C.: Office of Air Force History, USAF, 1991), 293 note 58.

10. Michael Gannon, *Operation Drumbeat* (New York: Harper & Row Publishers, 1990), 167.

11. Schaffel, *Emerging Shield,* 39.

12. Clay Blair, *Hitler's U-Boat War: The Hunters, 1939–1942* (New York: Random House, 1996), 505.

13. David Irving, *Hitler's War* (New York: The Viking Press, 1977), 186.

14. Andreas Nielsen, *The German Air Force General Staff* (New York: Arno Press, 1959), 152.

15. Herbert Molloy Mason Jr., *The Rise of the Luftwaffe 1918–1940* (New York: The Dial Press, 1973), 183.

16. Ibid., 184.

17. Ibid.

18. R. J. Overy, "From 'Uralbomber' to 'Amerikabomber': The Luftwaffe and Strategic Bombing," *The Journal of Strategic Studies,* 1, 2 (September 1978): 155.

19. Mason, *Rise of the Luftwaffe,* 185–186.

20. "Memorandum by the Chief of the Air Staff on Air Power Requirements of the Empire," Great Britain, Cabinet Papers, CAB 24/71, 9 December 1918, as quoted in Donald Kagan and Frederick W. Kagan, *While America Sleeps* (New York: St. Martin's Press, 2000), 19–20.

21. Irving, *Rise and Fall,* 46–47.

22. Ibid., 43.

23. Mason, Rise of the Luftwaffe, 214.

24. Manfred Griehl and Joachim Dressel, *German Heavy Bombers* (Atglen, PA: Schiffer Publishing Ltd., 1994), 6–8.

25. Benjamin King and Timothy Kutta, I*mpact: The History of Germany's V-Weapons in World War II* (Rockville Centre, NY: Sarpedon, 1998), 76.

26. Irving, *Rise and Fall,* 54.

27. Heinz J. Nowarra, *Junkers: Ju 290, Ju 390, etc.* (Atglen, PA: Schiffer Publishing, 1997), 14–16.

28. Albert Speer, *Inside the Third Reich: Memoirs* (New York: Macmillan Publishing Co., 1970), 346.

29. King and Kutta, *Impact,* 76.

30. Mason, *Rise of the Luftwaffe,* 199.

31. Irving, *Rise and Fall,* 170.

32. David Mondey, *The Concise Guide to Axis Aircraft of World War II* (London: Chancellor Press, 1996), 95–96.

33. Ibid., 150–151.

34. Gerhard L. Weinberg, *Germany, Hitler and World War II* (New York: Cambridge University Press, 1996), 196–197.

35. Gerhard L. Weinberg, *A World at Arms* (New York: Cambridge University Press, 1994), 178.

36. Norman J. W. Goda, *Tomorrow the World* (College Station: Texas A&M University Press, 1998), 27.

37. The most complete in-depth history of the Me 264 can be found in a series of articles written by Manfred Griehl in 1996 for the German publication *Flugzeug.* A briefer version can be found on the excellent website www.luft46.com.

38. Mondey, *Concise Guide,* 73–74.

39. Nowarra, *Junkers,* 11–12.

40. Mondey, *Concise Guide,* 130–131.

41. Norman Polmar and Thomas B. Allen, *World War II: America at War 1941–1945* (New York: Random House, 1991), 455.

42. Irving, *Rise and Fall,* 280.

43. www.warbirdsresourcegroup.org

44. Dan Johnson, www.luft46.com.

45. For the complete history of the Horten brothers and the Ho 18, as well as all their other amazing aircraft, I recommend David Myhra, *The Horten Brothers and Their All-Wing Aircraft* (Atglen, PA: Schiffer Publishing, 1999).

### Chapter 5: Rockets, Missiles, and the Nazi Icbm

1. Benjamin King and Timothy Kutta, *Impact: The History of Germany's V Weapons in World War II* (Rockville Centre, NY: Sarpedon Publishers, 1998), 48.
2. Michael J. Neufeld, *The Rocket and the Reich* (New York: Free Press, 1995), 7.
3. Two excellent histories of rocket development in prewar Germany are Willy Ley, *Rockets, Missiles, and Men in Space* (New York: Viking Press, 1968), and Frederick I. Ordway III and Mitchell R. Sharpe, *The Rocket Team* (New York: Thomas Y. Crowell Publishers, 1979).
4. Wernher von Braun, "Stellungnahme," June 27, 1935, National Air and Space Museum, Fort Eustis #746, as quoted in Neufeld, *The Rocket*, 46.
5. Ordway and Sharpe, *Rocket Team*, 25.
6. Norman Polmar and Thomas B. Allen, *World War II: America at War 1941–1945* (New York: Random House, 1991), 860–861; Louis L. Snyder, *Louis L. Snyder's Historical Guide to World War II* (Westport, CT: Greenwood Press, 1982), 731– 732.
7. Polmar and Allen, *World War II,* 861.
8. Ian V. Hogg, *German Secret Weapons of the Second World War* (Mechanicsburg, PA: Stackpole Books, 1999), 17–19.
9. King and Kutta, *Impact,* 94.
10. Martyn D. Tagg, "Airplanes, Combat and Maintenance Crews, and Air Bases," *U.S. Air Force Report.*
11. Smithsonian website, www.nasm.si.edu.
12. Majorie Kellogg-Van Rheeden, "Willy Fiedler, the Boy Who Wanted to Fly," Los Altos Town Crier, February 11, 1998.
13. Ordway and Sharpe, *Rocket Team,* 24; Ley, *Rockets,* 185.
14. Ley, *Rockets,* 188.
15. Walter Dornberger, *V-2* (New York: The Viking Press, 1954), 48.
16. Ley, *Rockets,* 218.
17. Neufeld, *The Rocket,* 92–93.
18. Ordway and Sharpe, *Rocket Team,* 57.
19. Dornberger, *V-2,* 142.
20. Neufeld, *The Rocket,* 138.
21. Ibid.
22. Dornberger, *V-2,* 142.
23. Neufeld, *The Rocket,* 139–141.
24. Dornberger, *V-2,* 143.
25. Ordway and Sharpe, *Rocket Team,* 56–57.
26. Dornberger, *V-2,* 250–251.
27. Ordway and Sharpe, *Rocket Team,* 57.
28. Albert Speer, *Inside the Third Reich* (New York: Macmillan, 1970), 437.
29. Neufeld, *The Rocket,* 176–184.
30. Ibid., 186–189.
31. Martin Gilbert, *The Second World War* (New York: Henry Holt & Company, 1989), 453.
32. Neufeld, *The Rocket,* 200–201.
33. Speer, Inside, 444–445; Neufeld, *The Rocket,* 201.

34. Correspondence to the author from Dr. Wagner of the Austria Federal Ministry of the Interior; website for the Mauthausen Concentration Camp Memorial, www.mauthausen-memorial.at.

35. King and Kutta, *Impact,* 72.

36. Brett Davis, "V-2 Plant Survivors Publicize Their Story," *The Huntsville* (AL) *Times,* February 28, 2000.

37. King and Kutta, *Impact,* 108–112.

38. Ibid., 104.

39. Jack Olsen, *Aphrodite: Desperate Mission* (New York: G. P. Putnam's Sons, 1970).

40. Ibid., 255.

41. As quoted in ibid., 16.

42. David Irving, *The Mare's Nest* (Boston: Little, Brown & Co., 1965), 219–220.

43. James McGovern, *Crossbow and Overcast* (New York: William Morrow & Co., 1964), 151–176.

44. Ley, *Rockets,* 236.

## Chapter 6: U-Boats to America

1. "The War Diary of the Operations Division, German Naval Staff," March 22, 1941, as cited in Gerhard L. Weinberg, *World in the Balance* (Hanover, NH: University Press of New England, 1981), 85.

2. Clay Blair, Hitler's *U-Boat War: The Hunters, 1939–1942* (New York: Random House, 1996), 443f.

3. Donald Sommerville, *World War II Day by Day* (Greenwich, CT: Brompton Books, 1989), 106.

4. Jeffrey M. Dorwart, *Conflict of Duty* (Annapolis: U.S. Naval Institute Press, 1983), 152.

5. Martin Gilbert, *The Second World War* (New York: Henry Holt & Co., 1989), 192.

6. Norman Polmar and Thomas B. Allen, *World War II* (New York: Random House, 1991), 258.

7. "U.S. Naval Administration in World War II: The Office of Naval Intelligence," 78–82, Naval Historical Division, Operational Archives, as cited in Dorwart, *Conflict,* 153.

8. Blair, *Hitler's U-Boat War,* 455.

9. John Toland, *Adolf Hitler* (New York: Ballantine Books, 1977), 951–952; Alan Bullock, *Hitler: A Study in Tyranny* (New York: Konecky & Konecky, 1999), 661–663.

10. Bullock, *Hitler,* 662.

11. William L. Shirer, *The Rise and Fall of the Third Reich: A History of Nazi Germany* (New York: Simon & Schuster, 1960), 894.

12. Weinberg, *World in the Balance,* 95.

13. Michael Gannon, *Operation Drumbeat* (New York: Harper & Row, 1990), xvi.

14. Details of the attack can be found in Zenji Orita and Joseph D. Harrington, I-Boat Captain (Canoga Park, CA: Major Books, 1976), 48–89. Radio Tokyo's reaction is in John J. Stephan, *Hawaii under the Rising Sun* (Honolulu: University of Hawaii Press, 1984), 125.

15. Gilbert, *Second World War,* 336.

16. Orita and Harrington, *I-Boat Captain,* 122–126; William H. Langenberg, "Japan Bombs the West Coast," *Aviation History* 10, 2 (November 1998).

17. Samuel Eliot Morison, *The Battle of the Atlantic 1939–1943* (Edison, NJ: Castle Books, 2001), 145.

18. *The New York Times,* January 21, 1945.

19. "The War Diary of the Operations Division, German Naval Staff," December 9, 1941, as quoted in Gannon, *Drumbeat,* 97–98.

20. George C. Marshall Research Library, Lexington, Virginia; Marshall Papers, Box 73, Folder 12, "King, Ernest J., 1942 May–1942 August," June 19, 1942, as quoted in Ernest J. King and Walter Muir Whitehill, *Fleet Admiral King: A Naval Record* (New York: W. W. Norton & Company, 1952), 455–456; also in Gannon, *Drumbeat,* 390–391.

21. "Training Manual," Naval Air Station, Quonset Point, Rhode Island, as quoted in Morison, *Battle of the Atlantic,* 127–128.

22. Gilbert, *Second World War,* 290, 304.

23. "War Record of the Fifth Naval District, 1942," 12–14, 460, Operational Archives, U.S. Naval Historical Center, as quoted in Gannon, *Drumbeat,* 380.

24. "War Diary, Eastern Sea Frontier," April 1942, 320–323. Naval Historical Division, Operational Archives, as cited in Gannon, Drumbeat, 380–381. Also in Morison, *Battle of the Atlantic,* 155.

25. Eugene Rachlis, *They Came to Kill* (New York: Random House, 1961); Theodore Taylor, *Fire on the Beaches* (New York: W. W. Norton, 1958).

26. Walter Dornberger, *V-2* (New York: Viking Press, 1954), 245–246.

27. Norman Polmar, *Atomic Submarines* (Princeton, NJ: Van Nostrand & Co., 1963), 197.

28. Ibid, 197.

29. James P. Hamill, "Launching the A4 (V2) Rocket Missile at Sea," Tech Report 16, Fort Bliss, Texas: Research and Development Service Sub-Office (rocket), August 7, 1946, as cited in Frederick I. Ordway III and Mitchell R. Sharpe, *The Rocket Team* (New York: Thomas Y. Crowell, 1979), 55.

30. Test Stand XII documents in Deutsches Museum Munich, GD639.3.4, as cited in Michael J. Neufeld, *The Rocket and the Reich* (New York: Free Press, 1995), 255.

31. Ordway and Sharpe, *Rocket Team,* 55.

32. Polmar, *Atomic Submarines,* 197–199.

33. Neufeld, *The Rocket,* 255.

34. Ordway and Sharpe, *Rocket Team,* 55.

35. Neufeld, *The Rocket,* 101.

36. Ibid., 191.

37. Ian V. Hogg, *German Secret Weapons of the Second World War* (Mechanicsburg, PA: Stackpole Books, 1999), 160.

38. Polmar, *Atomic Submarines,* 183.

39. Dornberger, *V-2,* 245–246.

40. Ibid., 184.

41. Blair, *Hitler's U-Boat War,* 680.

42. Gunter Hessler, "German Naval History: The U-Boat War in the Atlantic, 1939–1945" (London: Ministry of Defence—Navy, 1983), Section 3, 97, as cited in Philip K. Lundeberg, "Operation Teardrop Revisited," in Timothy J. Runyan and Jan M. Copes, eds., *To Die Gallantly: The Battle of the Atlantic* (Boulder, CO: Westview Press, 1994), 211.

43. *New York Times*, January 8, 1945, 1.

44. Blair, *Hitler's U-Boat War*, 683.

45. Ibid., 683.

46. German Navy/U-Boat Messages, SRGN 47404 of 2030/2 April 1945, Record Group 457 (National Security Agency), National Archives, Washington, D.C., as quoted in Lundeberg, "Teardrop," 212.

47. Blair, *Hitler's U-Boat War*, 686; Lundeberg, "Teardrop," 210.

48. Blair, *Hitler's U-Boat War*, 689.

49. Lundeberg, "Teardrop," 213.

50. "Irregularities Connected with the Handling of Surrendered German Submarines and Prisoners of War at the Navy Yard, Portsmouth, New Hampshire," SecNav/CNO file A16-2(3) EF30, Record Group 80, National Archives, as cited in Lundeberg, "Teardrop," 227.

### Chapter 7: Target: New York City

1. Thomas Powers, *Heisenberg's War* (New York: Alfred A. Knopf, 1993), 514.

2. Albert Speer, *Inside the Third Reich: Memoirs* (New York: Macmillan, 1970), 269.

3. Powers, *Heisenberg's War*, 147–148; Speer, Inside, 269–271.

4. David Irving, *The German Atomic Bomb* (New York: Simon & Schuster, 1967), 236fn.

5. Ronald H. Bailey, *The Air War in Europe* (Chicago: Time-Life Books, 1981), 132; Dr. Alfred Price, *Luftwaffe: Birth, Life & Death of an Air Force* (New York: Ballantine Books, 1969), 120–125.

6. Bailey, *Air War in Europe*, 132; Price, *Luftwaffe*, 120–125.

7. David Mondey, *The Concise Guide to Axis Aircraft of World War II* (London: Chancellor Press, 1996), 45–46.

8. Ibid., 22–23.

9. Gerhard L. Weinberg, *A World at Arms* (New York: Cambridge University Press, 1994), 1033 n.96.

10. Heinz J. Nowarra, *Junkers: Ju 290, Ju 390, etc.* (Atglen, PA: Schiffer Publishing, 1997), 45–46.

11. Dr. Alfred Price, *The Luftwaffe Data Book* (London: Greenhill Books, 1997), 94, 126.

12. Complete details of Kenneth P. Werrell's research into the Ju-390 flight to New York, as well as the alleged flights of Ju-290s to Manchuria, can be found in his "World War II German Long Distance Flights: Fraud or Record?," *Aerospace Historian* 35, 2 (Summer/June 1988).

13. *(London) Daily Telegraph*, September 2, 1969, 13.

14. Walter Hubatsch, Hitlers Weisungen fur die Hreigfuhrung 1939–1945, Dokumente des Oberkommandos der Wehrmacht (Frankfurt, 1962), 72–75, as cited in Holger H. Herwig, *Politics of Frustration: The United States in German Naval Planning, 1889–1941* (Boston: Little, Brown & Co., 1976), 212f.

15. William L. Shirer, *The Rise and Fall of the Third Reich: A History of Nazi Germany* (New York: Simon & Schuster, 1960), 817.
16. Prosecution Document 376-PS, Exhibit USA-161, International Military Tribunal, December 10, 1945, 389. The full text can be found at The Mazal Library, online at www.mazal.org. Letter cited in Gunter Moltmann, "Weltherrschaftsideen Hitlers," *Europa und Ubersee Festschrift fur Egmont Zechlin* (Hamburg: 1961). Also cited in Herwig, *Politics of Frustration*, 214 n.50.
17. Bundesarchiv/Militararchiv (Freiburg) RM 6/73, 22, September 1940, as cited in Norman J. W. Goda, *Tomorrow the World: Hitler, Northwest Africa, and the Path toward America* (College Station: Texas A&M University Press, 1998), 116–117.
18. Bundesarchiv/Militararchiv (Freiburg) PG 31748 Case 277, as cited in Herwig, *Politics of Frustration*, 214. Also see Percy Ernst Schramm, ed., *Kriegstagebuch des Oberkommandos der Wehrmacht*, 1: 15 (November 1940), as cited in Goda, *Tomorrow*, 120–121.
19. Goda, *Tomorrow*, 261, note 34.
20. Fuhrer Conferences on Naval Affairs, 1941, 57, as cited in Shirer, *Rise and Fall*, 879.
21. Ibid., 94, as cited in Shirer, *Rise and Fall*, 879.
22. Samuel Eliot Morison, *The Battle of the Atlantic 1939–1943* (Edison, NJ: Castle Books, 2001), 66–67.
23. Ibid.

### Chapter 8: Dr. Sanger's Space Bomber

1. David Baker, Ph.D., *The History of Manned Space Flight* (New York: Crown Publishers, 1982), 16.
2. Ibid., 16; Willy Ley, *Rockets, Missiles, and Men in Space* (New York: Viking Press, 1968), 547.
3. Ley, *Rockets,* 427.
4. Helmut Muller, "The High-Flying Legacy of Eugene Sanger," *Air & Space Smithsonian* (August/September 1987), 96.
5. Ibid.
6. Ley, *Rockets,* 444–445.
7. Baker, *Manned Space Flight,* 17.
8. Ley, *Rockets,* 447.
9. Ibid., 444.
10. Ibid., 445.

### Chapter 9: Invasion from the South

1. Holger H. Herwig, *Politics of Frustration* (Boston: Little, Brown & Co., 1976), 68.
2. Ibid., 68–69.
3. Ibid., 70–72.
4. Martin Gilbert, *The First World War: A Complete History* (New York: Henry Holt and Company, 1994), 308.
5. William L. Shirer, *Berlin Diary* (New York: Alfred A. Knopf, 1941), 474.

6. William Stevenson, *A Man Called Intrepid* (New York: Harcourt, Brace, Jovanovich, 1976), 297–298.

7. John Gunther, *Inside Latin America* (New York: Harper & Bros., 1941), 16.

8. Jeffrey M. Dorwart, *Conflict of Duty* (Annapolis: U.S. Naval Institute Press, 1983), 128.

9. Gunther, *Inside,* 16–19.

10. *The New York Times,* September 24, 1940, 8.

11. Gunther, *Inside,* 18–20.

12. Samuel Eliot Morison, *The Battle of the Atlantic 1939–1943* (Edison, NJ: Castle Books, 2001), 30–32.

13. Ibid.

14. Gunther, *Inside,* 351.

15. Ibid., 380–381.

16. Quoted in Theresa L. Kraus, "Planning the Defense of the South Atlantic: 1939–41: Securing Brazil," in Timothy J. Runyan and Jan M. Copes, eds., *To Die Gallantly* (Boulder, CO: Westview Press, 1994), 63.

17. Robert Shogan, *Hard Bargain* (New York: Scribners, 1995), 195.

18. "Denies Sending Troops," *The New York Times,* June 4, 1940, 12, col. 4.

19. John F. Bratzel, "Brazil, Espionage, and Donitz's Dream," in Runyan and Copes, *To Die,* 67.

20. For an interesting and well-researched history of the planned seizure and occupation of northeastern Brazil, see Michael Gannon, "Invade Brazil?!" *U.S. Naval Institute Proceedings* 125, 160 (October 1999): 58–65.

*Chapter 10: Italy Targets New York*

1. Winston S. Churchill, *Memoirs of the Second World War* (New York: Bonanza Books, 1978), 503.

2. Clay Blair, *Hitler's U-Boat War: The Hunters 1939–1942* (New York: Random House, 1996), 396–397; Janusz Piekalkiewicz, *Sea War 1939–1945* (New York: Sterling Publishing, 1987), 172–173.

3. Blair, *Hitler's U-Boat War,* 399. J. Valerio Borghese, *Sea Devils* (Chicago: Henry Regnery & Co., 1954), 131.

4. Borghese, *Sea Devils,* 263.

5. Antonio Bragadin, *The Italian Navy in World War II* (Annapolis: U.S. Naval Institute, 1957), 279.

6. Ibid., 284–286; Borghese, *Sea Devils,* 138–156; Piekalkiewicz, *Sea War,* 179–181; Churchill, *Memoirs,* 504.

7. Jonathan W. Thompson, *Italian Civil and Military Aircraft 1930–1945* (New York: Aero Publishers, 1963), 62–64; Giancarlo Garello, "Target: New York, Italian Planned Raids to United States," *Aerofan* 15, 62 (September 1997): 146.

8. Norman Polmar and Thomas B. Allen, *World War II: America at War 1941–1945* (New York: Random House, 1991), 548.

9. Borghese, *Sea Devils,* 23.

10. Clay Blair, *Hitler's U-Boat War*, 230.
11. Borghese, *Sea Devils*, 200.
12. Bragadin, *Italian Navy*, 288.
13. Paul Kemp, *Underwater Warriors* (London: Cassell & Co., 2000), 59.
14. Blair, *Hitler's U-Boat War*, 230.
15. Borghese, *Sea Devils*, 261.
16. Garello, "Target: New York," 132–149.

### *Chapter 11: Why They Failed*

1. Richard Overy, *Why the Allies Won* (New York: W. W. Norton & Co., 1996), 104.
2. Dr. Alfred Price, *Luftwaffe: Birth, Life & Death of an Air Force* (New York: Ballantine Books, 1969), 77.
3. David Irving, *The Rise and Fall of the Luftwaffe: The Life of Field Marshal Erhard Milch* (Boston: Little, Brown & Co., 1973), 81.
4. Stephen Ambrose, *The Wild Blue: The Men and Boys Who Flew the B-24s over Germany* (New York: Simon & Schuster, 2001), 79.

# BIBLIOGRAPHY

**Books and Articles**

Allhoff, Fred. *Lightning in the Night.* Englewood Cliffs, NJ: Prentice-Hall, Inc., 1979.

Ambrose, Stephen E. *The Wild Blue: The Men and Boys Who Flew the B-24s over Germany.* New York: Simon & Schuster, 2001.

Bailey, Ronald H. *The Air War in Europe.* Chicago: Time-Life Books, 1981.

Bailey, Thomas A., and Paul Bryan. *Hitler vs. Roosevelt: The Undeclared Naval War.* New York: The Free Press, 1979.

Baker, David, Ph.D. *The History of Manned Space Flight.* New York: Crown Publishers, 1982.

Below, Nicolaus von. *At Hitler's Side.* London: Greenhill Books, 2001.

Blair, Clay. *Hitler's U-Boat War: The Hunted, 1942–1945.* New York: Random House, 1998.

———. *Hitler's U-Boat War: The Hunters, 1939–1942.* New York: Random House, 1996.

Borghese, J. Valerio. *Sea Devils.* Chicago: Henry Regnery & Co., 1954.

Bragadin, Antonio. *The Italian Navy in World War II.* Annapolis: U.S. Naval Institute, 1957.

Bratzel, John F. "Brazil, Espionage, and Donitz's Dream." In Timothy J. Runyan and Jan M. Copes, eds., *To Die Gallantly.* Boulder, CO: Westview Press, 1994.

Breuer, William B. *Secret Weapons of World War II.* New York: John Wiley & Sons, 2000.

———. *Top Secret Tales of World War II.* New York: John Wiley & Sons, 2000.

Buchanan, Patrick J. *A Republic, Not an Empire.* Washington, D.C.: Regnery & Co., 1999.

Bullock, Alan. *Hitler: A Study in Tyranny.* New York: Konecky & Konecky, 1999.

Burleigh, Michael. *The Third Reich: A New History.* New York: Hill and Wang, 2000.

Carter, Lt. A. "It Can Be Done." *Canadian Defence Quarterly* 16 (October 1938): 54.

Childs, Marquis W. "London Wins The Battle." *The National Geographic Magazine* 88, 2 (August, 1945): 129.

Churchill, Winston S. *Memoirs of the Second World War.* New York: Bonanza Books, 1978.

Compton, James V. *The Swastika and the Eagle.* Boston: Houghton Mifflin Co., 1967.

Dallek, Robert. *Franklin D. Roosevelt and American Foreign Policy, 1939–1945.* New York: Oxford University Press, 1979.

Davis, Brett. "V-2 Plant Survivors Publicize Their Story." *The Huntsville (AL) Times* (February 28, 2000).

De Toledano, Ralph. *J. Edgar Hoover: The Man and His Time.* New Rochelle, NY: Arlington House, 1973.

Dorman, Michael. *The Secret Service Story.* New York: Delacorte Press, 1967.

Dornberger, Walter. *V-2.* New York: Viking Press, 1954.

Dorwart, Jeffrey M. *Conflict of Duty.* Annapolis: U.S. Naval Institute Press, 1983.

Dunnigan, James F., and Albert A. Nofi. *Dirty Little Secrets of World War II.* New York: William Morrow & Co., 1994.

Fischer, Klaus P. *Nazi Germany: A New History.* New York: Continuum Publishing, 1995.

Ford, Brian. *German Secret Weapons: Blueprint for Mars.* New York: Ballantine Books, 1969.

Gannon, Michael. *Operation Drumbeat.* New York: Harper & Row Publishers, 1990.

———. "Invade Brazil?!" *Proceedings* 125, 160 (October 1990).

Garello, Giancarlo. "Target: New York, Italian Planned Raids to United States." *Aerofan* 15, 62 (September 1997).

Garlinski, Josef. *Hitler's Last Weapons.* London: Magnum Books, 1979.

Gilbert, Martin. *The Second World War.* New York: Henry Holt & Company, 1989.

———. *The First World War: A Complete History.* New York: Henry Holt and Company, 1994.

Goda, Norman J.W. *Tomorrow the World: Hitler, Northwest Africa, and the Path toward America.* College Station: Texas A&M University Press, 1998.

Griehl, Manfred. "The Banana Plane." *Flugzeug* (February 1996).

———. "A Dream Is Fading." *Flugzeug* (March 1996).

———. "The Me 264 V1." *Flugzeug* (April 1996).

Griehl, Manfred, and Joachim Dressel. *German Heavy Bombers.* Atglen, PA: Schiffer Publishing Ltd., 1994.

Grunberger, Richard. *The 12-Year Reich: A Social History of Nazi Germany 1933–1945.* New York: Holt, Rinehart and Winston, 1971.

Gunther, John. *Inside Latin America.* New York: Harper & Bros., 1941.

Hagan, Kenneth J. (ed). *In Peace and War.* Westport, CT: Greenwood Press, 1984.

Henshall, Philip. *Vengeance: Hitler's Nuclear Weapon, Fact or Fiction?* Gloucestershire: Sutton Publishing Ltd., 1995.

———. *The Nuclear Axis.* Gloucestershire: Sutton Publishing Ltd., 2000.

Herwig, Holger H. *Politics of Frustration: The United States in German Naval Planning, 1889–1941.* Boston: Little, Brown & Co., 1976.

Hirsch, Phil (ed.). *Great Untold Stories of World War II.* New York: Pyramid Books, 1968.

Hogg, Ian V. *German Secret Weapons of the Second World War.* Mechanicsburg, PA: Stackpole Books, 1999.

Hoyt, Edwin P. *U-Boats Offshore: When Hitler Struck America.* Briarcliff, NY: Stein & Day Publishers, 1978.

Irving, David. *The Mare's Nest.* Boston: Little, Brown & Co., 1965.

———. *The German Atomic Bomb.* New York: Simon & Schuster, 1967.

———. *The Rise and Fall of the Luftwaffe: The Life of Field Marshal Erhard Milch.* Boston: Little, Brown & Co., 1973.

———. *Hitler's War.* New York: Viking Press, 1977.

Jeffers, H. Paul. *Colonel Roosevelt: Theodore Roosevelt Goes to War 1897–1898.* New York: John Wiley & Sons, 1996.

Johnson, David. *V-1, V-2: Hitler's Vengeance on London.* Briarcliff, NY: Stein & Day Publishers, 1981.

Kagan, Donald, and Frederick W. Kagan. *While America Sleeps.* New York: St. Martin's Press, 2000.

Kahn, David. *Hitler's Spies: German Military Intelligence in World War II.* New York: Macmillan Publishing Co., 1978.

Kellogg-Van Rheeden, Marjorie. "Willy Fiedler, the Boy Who Wanted to Fly." *Los Altos Town Crier* (February 11, 1998).

Kemp, Paul. *Underwater Warriors.* London: Cassell & Company, 2000.

Kennett, Lee. *A History of Strategic Bombing.* New York: Scribner's Sons, 1982.

King, Benjamin, and Timothy Kutta. *Impact: The History of Germany's V-Weapons in World War II.* Rockville Centre, NY: Sarpedon Publishers, 1998.

King, Ernest J., and Walter Muir Whitehill. *Fleet Admiral King: A Naval Record.* New York: W. W. Norton & Co., 1952.

Kraus, Theresa L. "Planning the Defense of the South Atlantic: 1939–1941." In Timothy J. Runyan and Jan M. Copes, eds., *To Die Gallantly.* Boulder, CO: Westview Press, 1994.

Langenberg, William H. "Japan Bombs the West Coast." *Aviation History* 10, 2 (November 1998).

Ley, Willy. *Rockets, Missiles, and Men in Space.* New York: Viking Press, 1968.

Lundeberg, Philip K. "Operation Teardrop Revisited." In Timothy J. Runyan and Jan M. Copes, eds., *To Die Gallantly.* Boulder, CO: Westview Press, 1994.

Manno, Jack. *Arming the Heavens.* New York: Dodd, Mead & Co., 1984.

Mason, Herbert Molloy, Jr., *The Rise of the Luftwaffe 1918–1940.* New York: The Dial Press, 1973.

McGovern, James. *Crossbow and Overcast.* New York: William Morrow & Co., 1964.

Mondey, David. *The Concise Guide to Axis Aircraft of World War II.* London: Chancellor Press, 1996.

Morison, Samuel Eliot. *The Battle of the Atlantic 1939–1943.* Edison, NJ: Castle Books, 2001.

Muller, Helmut. "The High-Flying Legacy of Eugene Sanger." *Air & Space Smithsonian* (August/September 1987).

Murphy, Charles J. V. "Letter from Recife—Intrigue on the Bulge." *Fortune* (April 1941).

Myhra, David. *The Horten Brothers and Their All-Wing Aircraft.* Atglen, PA: Schiffer Publishing, 1999.

———. *Sanger: Germany's Orbital Rocket Bomber in World War II.* Atglen, PA: Schiffer Publishing, 2001.

Neufeld, Michael J. *The Rocket and the Reich.* New York: Free Press, 1995.

Nielsen, Andreas. *The German Air Force General Staff.* New York: Arno Press, 1959.

Nowarra, Heinz J. *Junkers: Ju 290, Ju 390, etc.* Atglen, PA: Schiffer Publishing, 1997.

Olsen, Jack. *Aphrodite: Desperate Mission*. New York: G. P. Putnam's Sons, 1970.

Ordway, Frederick I., III, and Mitchell R. Sharpe. *The Rocket Team*. New York: Thomas Y. Crowell Publishers, 1979.

Orita, Zenji, and Joseph D. Harrington. *I-Boat Captain*. Canoga Park, CA: Major Books, 1976.

O'Toole, G. J. A. *The Spanish War: An American Epic—1898*. New York: W. W. Norton, 1984.

Overy, R. J. "From 'Uralbomber' to 'Amerikabomber': The Luftwaffe and Strategic Bombing." *The Journal of Strategic Studies* 1, 2 (September 1978).

Overy, Richard. *Why the Allies Won*. New York: W. W. Norton & Co., 1996.

Parrish, Thomas (ed.). *The Simon & Schuster Encyclopedia of World War II*. New York: Simon & Schuster, 1978.

Peet, John. "Berlin Notebook." *German Democratic Report*, October 4, 1972.

Piekalkiewicz, Janusz. *Sea War 1939–1945*. New York: Sterling Publishing, 1987.

Pogue, Forrest C. *George C. Marshall*. 3 vols. New York: Viking Press, 1963–1973.

Polmar, Norman. *Atomic Submarines*. Princeton, NJ: Van Nostrand & Co., 1963.

Polmar, Norman, and Thomas B. Allen. *World War II: America at War 1941–1945*. New York: Random House, 1991.

Powers, Thomas. *Heisenberg's War*. New York: Alfred A. Knopf, 1993.

Price, Dr. Alfred. *Luftwaffe: Birth, Life & Death of an Air Force*. New York: Ballantine Books, 1969.

———. *The Luftwaffe Data Book*. London: Greenhill Books, 1997.

Rachlis, Eugene. *They Came to Kill*. New York: Random House, 1961.

Rees, Ed. *The Seas and the Subs*. New York: Duell, Sloan and Pearce, 1961.

Rich, Norman. *Hitler's War Aims*. New York: W. W. Norton, 1973.

"Robot Bomb Attack Feared." *New York Times* (January 21, 1945).

Runyan, Timothy J., and Jan M. Copes (eds.). *To Die Gallantly: The Battle of the Atlantic*. Boulder, CO: Westview Press, 1994.

Sargent, Nathan, USN. *Admiral Dewey and the Manila Campaign*. Washington, D.C.: Naval Historical Foundation, 1947.

Schaffel, Kenneth. *The Emerging Shield*. Washington, D.C.: Office of Air Force History, USAF, 1991.

Shepherd, Christopher. *German Aircraft of World War II*. Briarcliff Manor, NY: Stein & Day Publishers, 1976.

Shirer, William L. *Berlin Diary*. New York: Alfred A. Knopf, 1941.

———. *The Rise and Fall of the Third Reich: A History of Nazi Germany*. New York: Simon & Schuster, 1960.

Shogan, Robert. *Hard Bargain*. New York: Scribners, 1995.

Smith, George W. *Carlson's Raid*. Novato, CA: Presidio Press, 2001.

Snyder, Louis L. *Louis L. Snyder's Historical Guide to World War II*. Westport, CT: Greenwood Press, 1982.

Sommerville, Donald. *World War II Day by Day*. Greenwich, CT: Brompton Books, 1989.

Speer, Albert. *Inside the Third Reich: Memoirs.* New York: Macmillan Publishing Co., 1970.

Stephan, John J. *Hawaii under the Rising Sun.* Honolulu: University of Hawaii Press, 1984.

Stevenson, William. *A Man Called Intrepid.* New York: Harcourt, Brace, Jovanovich, 1976.

Sweetman, Bill. *Aurora: The Pentagon's Secret Hypersonic Spy Plane.* Osceola, WI: Motorbooks International, 1993.

Tagg, Martyn D. "Airplanes, Combat and Maintenance Crews, and Air Bases." *U.S. Air Force Report.* Alamogordo, NM: Holloman Air Force Base Cultural Resources Publication No. 6, 1998.

Taylor, Theodore. *Fire on the Beaches.* New York: W. W. Norton and Company, 1958.

Thompson, Jonathan W. *Italian Civil and Military Aircraft 1930–1945.* New York: Aero Publishers, 1963.

Toland, John. *Adolf Hitler.* New York: Ballantine Books, 1977.

Trevor-Roper, Hugh R. (ed.). *Hitler's Table Talk, 1941–1944.* London: Weidenfeld & Nicolson, 1953.

Weinberg, Gerhard L. (ed.). *Hitlers Zweites Buch: Ein Dokument aus dem Jahr 1928.* Stuttgart: Deutsche Verlags-Ansalt, 1961.

———. *World in the Balance: Behind the Scenes of World War II.* Hanover, NH: University Press of New England, 1981.

———. *A World at Arms.* New York: Cambridge University Press, 1994.

———. *Germany, Hitler, and World War II.* New York: Cambridge University Press, 1996.

———. *Hitler's Second Book.* New York: Enigma Books, 2003.

Werrell, Kenneth P. "World War II German Long Distance Flights: Fraud or Record?" *Aerospace Historian* 35, 2 (Summer/June 1988).

Young, Donald J. "West Coast War Zone." *World War II* 13, 2 (July 1998).

### Websites

A4/V2 Resource Site, www.v2rocket.com

Air and Sea Models, http://navismagazine.com

Air Model Products, www.airmodel.de

Aviation History, Technology and Airpower, www.danshistory.com

Beggs Aerospace, http://ouray.cudenver.edu/_wrbeggs/newindex.html

Eagle 3's Nest, www-personal.umich.edu/_buzznau/

Encyclopedia Astronautica, www.astronautix.com

German Militaria & Collectables, www.german-militaria.co.uk

German Naval History, www.german-navy.de

German VTO & Helicopter Projects of World War II, www.germanvtol.com

Giorgio Apostolo Editore Site, www.apostoloeditore.com

Haze Gray & Underway Naval History & Photography, www.hazegray.org

The History of Fort Tilden, www.geocities.com/fort_tilden/uboats.html
The History Net, www. historynet.com
Italy at War, www.comandosupremo.com
Japanese Aircraft & Ship Research Center, www.j-aircraft.com
Kingston Vacuum Works, www.warmplastic.com
Luft '46, www.luft46.com
Luftwaffe Resource Center, www.warbirdsresourcegroup.org
Mauthausen Concentration Camp Memorial, www.mauthausen-memorial.gv.at/
The Mazal Library, www.mazal.org
The Roseland Family Site, www.theroselands.com/usscusk
Science News Online, www.sciencenews.org
Smithsonian, www.nasm.si.edu
Space Frontier Foundation, www.space-frontier.org
Spaceline, Inc., www.spaceline.org
The Submarine Portal, www.subnetitalia.it
U-Boat.Net, www.uboat.net
The U-Boat War, www.uboatwar.net/
Vittorelli Edizioni, www.vittorelli.it
World War II in the Pacific, www.ww2pacific.com

# Index

Aimone of Spoleto, Duke (Italian Admiral), 150

Aircraft. *See* German aircraft; Italian aircraft; U.S. aircraft

Air War College (German), 45

Allhoff, Fred (*Lightning in the Night,* 1940), 41

Allied/British intelligence: A4 rockets, 91; *General Report on Aircraft Engines and Aircraft Equipment,* 125; Reginald V. Jones, 90–91; New York City missile attack plans, 114–15; Operation Hydra, 88–89, 91; Peenemunde surrenders, 92–94; Sandys, Duncan, 90–91; V-1/V-2, 91. *See also* Mission Aphrodite

Amedeo of Aosta, Duke (Italian Aviation General), 150

America. *See* United States

America Bomber, 43, 131–32; Focke-Wulf Aircraft Construction Company (German manufacturer), 62, 131–32; and Göring, 39–40; Heinkel (manufacturer), 60; Junkers Company (German aircraft manufacturer), 58; Messerschmitt long-range bomber claim, 40; and Willy Messerschmitt, 50–51, 133. *See also* He 277; Ho 18; Ju 390; Me 264; Silverbird Bomber (*Silbervogel*); Ta 400

America-Case (for bombing by Germany), 53–55

America Rocket (*Amerikarakette*), 85, 89–90, 119

Antipodal Bomber, 132–36

Aphrodite. *See* Mission Aphrodite

A rockets: A1, 78; A2, 78–79; A3, 80; A4, 81–84, 86–88, 91–94, 105; A9, 83–87, 132; A10, 85–87; A9/A10, 87, 88–90, 92; piloted version, 86. *See also* Rockets, German; V-2; Test Stand XII (V-2 U.S. attack plan)

Atmosphere Skipper, 132–36

Atomic fission Heisenberg lecture, 119–21

Azores attack plan, Maj. Sigismund Freiherr von Falkenstein memo, 127

Brauchitsch, Walther von. *See* von Bauchitsch, Field Marshal Walther (German Army Commander-in-Chief)

Baum, Alex (French resistance German POW), 90

Bayerische Flugzeugwerke. *See* Messerschmitt (German aircraft manufacturer)

Bin Laden, Osama, 13

Bismarck, German Chancellor Otto von, 138

Blohm and Voss (German aircraft manufacturer), 122–23. *See also* German aircraft, BV

# About the Author

James P. Duffy is a writer who specializes in military history. This is his fourteenth book.